DATE DUE 2 hour

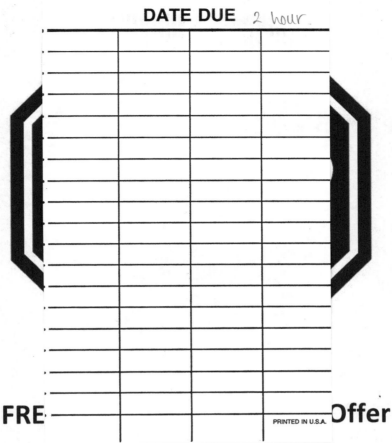

PRINTED IN U.S.A.

FRE————————————————**Offer**

To help us better serve you, we have developed a Test Taking Tips DVD that we would like to give you for FREE. **This DVD covers world-class test taking tips that you can use to be even more successful when you are taking your test.**

All that we ask is that you email us your feedback about your study guide. Please let us know what you thought about it – whether that is good, bad or indifferent.

To get your **FREE Test Taking Tips DVD**, email freedvd@studyguideteam.com with "FREE DVD" in the subject line and the following information in the body of the email:

  a. The title of your study guide.

  b. Your product rating on a scale of 1-5, with 5 being the highest rating.

  c. Your feedback about the study guide. What did you think of it?

  d. Your full name and shipping address to send your free DVD.

If you have any questions   s at
freedvd@studyguidetean

Thanks again!

LB 1762 .P73 2017
PRAXIS general science content
knowledge 5435 test prep

Praxis General Science Content Knowledge 5435 Test Prep

Praxis II General Science Content Knowledge 5435 Study Guide & Practice Test Questions

Test Prep Books Science Team

Table of Contents

Quick Overview

As you draw closer to taking your exam, effective preparation becomes more and more important. Thankfully, you have this study guide to help you get ready. Use this guide to help keep your studying on track and refer to it often.

This study guide contains several key sections that will help you be successful on your exam. The guide contains tips for what you should do the night before and the day of the test. Also included are test-taking tips. Knowing the right information is not always enough. Many well-prepared test takers struggle with exams. These tips will help equip you to accurately read, assess, and answer test questions.

A large part of the guide is devoted to showing you what content to expect on the exam and to helping you better understand that content. Near the end of this guide is a practice test so that you can see how well you have grasped the content. Then, answer explanations are provided so that you can understand why you missed certain questions.

Don't try to cram the night before you take your exam. This is not a wise strategy for a few reasons. First, your retention of the information will be low. Your time would be better used by reviewing information you already know rather than trying to learn a lot of new information. Second, you will likely become stressed as you try to gain a large amount of knowledge in a short amount of time. Third, you will be depriving yourself of sleep. So be sure to go to bed at a reasonable time the night before. Being well-rested helps you focus and remain calm.

Be sure to eat a substantial breakfast the morning of the exam. If you are taking the exam in the afternoon, be sure to have a good lunch as well. Being hungry is distracting and can make it difficult to focus. You have hopefully spent lots of time preparing for the exam. Don't let an empty stomach get in the way of success!

When travelling to the testing center, leave earlier than needed. That way, you have a buffer in case you experience any delays. This will help you remain calm and will keep you from missing your appointment time at the testing center.

Be sure to pace yourself during the exam. Don't try to rush through the exam. There is no need to risk performing poorly on the exam just so you can leave the testing center early. Allow yourself to use all of the allotted time if needed.

Remain positive while taking the exam even if you feel like you are performing poorly. Thinking about the content you should have mastered will not help you perform better on the exam.

Once the exam is complete, take some time to relax. Even if you feel that you need to take the exam again, you will be well served by some down time before you begin studying again. It's often easier to convince yourself to study if you know that it will come with a reward!

Test-Taking Strategies

1. Predicting the Answer

When you feel confident in your preparation for a multiple-choice test, try predicting the answer before reading the answer choices. This is especially useful on questions that test objective factual knowledge or that ask you to fill in a blank. By predicting the answer before reading the available choices, you eliminate the possibility that you will be distracted or led astray by an incorrect answer choice. You will feel more confident in your selection if you read the question, predict the answer, and then find your prediction among the answer choices. After using this strategy, be sure to still read all of the answer choices carefully and completely. If you feel unprepared, you should not attempt to predict the answers. This would be a waste of time and an opportunity for your mind to wander in the wrong direction.

2. Reading the Whole Question

Too often, test takers scan a multiple-choice question, recognize a few familiar words, and immediately jump to the answer choices. Test authors are aware of this common impatience, and they will sometimes prey upon it. For instance, a test author might subtly turn the question into a negative, or he or she might redirect the focus of the question right at the end. The only way to avoid falling into these traps is to read the entirety of the question carefully before reading the answer choices.

3. Looking for Wrong Answers

Long and complicated multiple-choice questions can be intimidating. One way to simplify a difficult multiple-choice question is to eliminate all of the answer choices that are clearly wrong. In most sets of answers, there will be at least one selection that can be dismissed right away. If the test is administered on paper, the test taker could draw a line through it to indicate that it may be ignored; otherwise, the test taker will have to perform this operation mentally or on scratch paper. In either case, once the obviously incorrect answers have been eliminated, the remaining choices may be considered. Sometimes identifying the clearly wrong answers will give the test taker some information about the correct answer. For instance, if one of the remaining answer choices is a direct opposite of one of the eliminated answer choices, it may well be the correct answer. The opposite of obviously wrong is obviously right! Of course, this is not always the case. Some answers are obviously incorrect simply because they are irrelevant to the question being asked. Still, identifying and eliminating some incorrect answer choices is a good way to simplify a multiple-choice question.

4. Don't Overanalyze

Anxious test takers often overanalyze questions. When you are nervous, your brain will often run wild, causing you to make associations and discover clues that don't actually exist. If you feel that this may be a problem for you, do whatever you can to slow down during the test. Try taking a deep breath or counting to ten. As you read and consider the question, restrict yourself to the particular words used by the author. Avoid thought tangents about what the author *really* meant, or what he or she was *trying* to say. The only things that matter on a multiple-choice test are the words that are actually in the question. You must avoid reading too much into a multiple-choice question, or supposing that the writer meant something other than what he or she wrote.

5. No Need for Panic

It is wise to learn as many strategies as possible before taking a multiple-choice test, but it is likely that you will come across a few questions for which you simply don't know the answer. In this situation, avoid panicking. Because most multiple-choice tests include dozens of questions, the relative value of a single wrong answer is small. Moreover, your failure on one question has no effect on your success elsewhere on the test. As much as possible, you should compartmentalize each question on a multiple-choice test. In other words, you should not allow your feelings about one question to affect your success on the others. When you find a question that you either don't understand or don't know how to answer, just take a deep breath and do your best. Read the entire question slowly and carefully. Try rephrasing the question a couple of different ways. Then, read all of the answer choices carefully. After eliminating obviously wrong answers, make a selection and move on to the next question.

6. Confusing Answer Choices

When working on a difficult multiple-choice question, there may be a tendency to focus on the answer choices that are the easiest to understand. Many people, whether consciously or not, gravitate to the answer choices that require the least concentration, knowledge, and memory. This is a mistake. When you come across an answer choice that is confusing, you should give it extra attention. A question might be confusing because you do not know the subject matter to which it refers. If this is the case, don't eliminate the answer before you have affirmatively settled on another. When you come across an answer choice of this type, set it aside as you look at the remaining choices. If you can confidently assert that one of the other choices is correct, you can leave the confusing answer aside. Otherwise, you will need to take a moment to try to better understand the confusing answer choice. Rephrasing is one way to tease out the sense of a confusing answer choice.

7. Your First Instinct

Many people struggle with multiple-choice tests because they overthink the questions. If you have studied sufficiently for the test, you should be prepared to trust your first instinct once you have carefully and completely read the question and all of the answer choices. There is a great deal of research suggesting that the mind can come to the correct conclusion very quickly once it has obtained all of the relevant information. At times, it may seem to you as if your intuition is working faster even than your reasoning mind. This may in fact be true. The knowledge you obtain while studying may be retrieved from your subconscious before you have a chance to work out the associations that support it. Verify your instinct by working out the reasons that it should be trusted.

8. Key Words

Many test takers struggle with multiple-choice questions because they have poor reading comprehension skills. Quickly reading and understanding a multiple-choice question requires a mixture of skill and experience. To help with this, try jotting down a few key words and phrases on a piece of scrap paper. Doing this concentrates the process of reading and forces the mind to weigh the relative importance of the question's parts. In selecting words and phrases to write down, the test taker thinks about the question more deeply and carefully. This is especially true for multiple-choice questions that are preceded by a long prompt.

9. Subtle Negatives

One of the oldest tricks in the multiple-choice test writer's book is to subtly reverse the meaning of a question with a word like *not* or *except*. If you are not paying attention to each word in the question, you can easily be led astray by this trick. For instance, a common question format is, "Which of the following is...?" Obviously, if the question instead is, "Which of the following is not...?," then the answer will be quite different. Even worse, the test makers are aware of the potential for this mistake and will include one answer choice that would be correct if the question were not negated or reversed. A test taker who misses the reversal will find what he or she believes to be a correct answer and will be so confident that he or she will fail to reread the question and discover the original error. The only way to avoid this is to practice a wide variety of multiple-choice questions and to pay close attention to each and every word.

10. Reading Every Answer Choice

It may seem obvious, but you should always read every one of the answer choices! Too many test takers fall into the habit of scanning the question and assuming that they understand the question because they recognize a few key words. From there, they pick the first answer choice that answers the question they believe they have read. Test takers who read all of the answer choices might discover that one of the latter answer choices is actually *more* correct. Moreover, reading all of the answer choices can remind you of facts related to the question that can help you arrive at the correct answer. Sometimes, a misstatement or incorrect detail in one of the latter answer choices will trigger your memory of the subject and will enable you to find the right answer. Failing to read all of the answer choices is like not reading all of the items on a restaurant menu: you might miss out on the perfect choice.

11. Spot the Hedges

One of the keys to success on multiple-choice tests is paying close attention to every word. This is never more true than with words like *almost*, *most*, *some*, and *sometimes*. These words are called "hedges" because they indicate that a statement is not totally true or not true in every place and time. An absolute statement will contain no hedges, but in many subjects, like literature and history, the answers are not always straightforward or absolute. There are always exceptions to the rules in these subjects. For this reason, you should favor those multiple-choice questions that contain hedging language. The presence of qualifying words indicates that the author is taking special care with his or her words, which is certainly important when composing the right answer. After all, there are many ways to be wrong, but there is only one way to be right! For this reason, it is wise to avoid answers that are absolute when taking a multiple-choice test. An absolute answer is one that says things are either all one way or all another. They often include words like *every*, *always*, *best*, and *never*. If you are taking a multiple-choice test in a subject that doesn't lend itself to absolute answers, be on your guard if you see any of these words.

12. Long Answers

In many subject areas, the answers are not simple. As already mentioned, the right answer often requires hedges. Another common feature of the answers to a complex or subjective question are qualifying clauses, which are groups of words that subtly modify the meaning of the sentence. If the question or answer choice describes a rule to which there are exceptions or the subject matter is complicated, ambiguous, or confusing, the correct answer will require many words in order to be expressed clearly and accurately. In essence, you should not be deterred by answer choices that seem excessively long. Oftentimes, the author of the text will not be able to write the correct answer without offering some qualifications and modifications. Your job is to read the answer choices thoroughly and completely and to select the one that most accurately and precisely answers the question.

13. Restating to Understand

Sometimes, a question on a multiple-choice test is difficult not because of what it asks but because of how it is written. If this is the case, restate the question or answer choice in different words. This process serves a couple of important purposes. First, it forces you to concentrate on the core of the question. In order to rephrase the question accurately, you have to understand it well. Rephrasing the question will concentrate your mind on the key words and ideas. Second, it will present the information to your mind in a fresh way. This process may trigger your memory and render some useful scrap of information picked up while studying.

14. True Statements

Sometimes an answer choice will be true in itself, but it does not answer the question. This is one of the main reasons why it is essential to read the question carefully and completely before proceeding to the answer choices. Too often, test takers skip ahead to the answer choices and look for true statements. Having found one of these, they are content to select it without reference to the question above. Obviously, this provides an easy way for test makers to play tricks. The savvy test taker will always read the entire question before turning to the answer choices. Then, having settled on a correct answer choice, he or she will refer to the original question and ensure that the selected answer is relevant. The mistake of choosing a correct-but-irrelevant answer choice is especially common on questions related to specific pieces of objective knowledge, like historical or scientific facts. A prepared test taker will have a wealth of factual knowledge at his or her disposal, and should not be careless in its application.

15. No Patterns

One of the more dangerous ideas that circulates about multiple-choice tests is that the correct answers tend to fall into patterns. These erroneous ideas range from a belief that B and C are the most common right answers, to the idea that an unprepared test-taker should answer "A-B-A-C-A-D-A-B-A." It cannot be emphasized enough that pattern-seeking of this type is exactly the WRONG way to approach a multiple-choice test. To begin with, it is highly unlikely that the test maker will plot the correct answers according to some predetermined pattern. The questions are scrambled and delivered in a random order. Furthermore, even if the test maker was following a pattern in the assignation of correct answers, there is no reason why the test taker would know which pattern he or she was using. Any attempt to discern a pattern in the answer choices is a waste of time and a distraction from the real work of taking the test. A test taker would be much better served by extra preparation before the test than by reliance on a pattern in the answers.

FREE DVD OFFER

Don't forget that doing well on your exam includes both understanding the test content and understanding how to use what you know to do well on the test. We offer a completely FREE Test Taking Tips DVD that covers world class test taking tips that you can use to be even more successful when you are taking your test.

All that we ask is that you email us your feedback about your study guide. To get your **FREE Test Taking Tips DVD**, email freedvd@studyguideteam.com with "FREE DVD" in the subject line and the following information in the body of the email:

- The title of your study guide.
- Your product rating on a scale of 1-5, with 5 being the highest rating.
- Your feedback about the study guide. What did you think of it?
- Your full name and shipping address to send your free DVD.

Introduction

Function of the Test

The Praxis II General Science Content Knowledge exam is one of the Educational Testing Service's (ETS's) Subject Assessment tests. The Subject Assessment tests are intended to measure knowledge of more than ninety specific subjects taught by educators in kindergarten through twelfth grade classrooms, as well as the knowledge of teaching skills for those subject areas. The tests are offered worldwide, but are primarily used in the United States, where they are typically a required component of the certification and licensing procedure in certain states. They are also used as part of the licensing process by some professional associations and organizations.

The General Science Content Knowledge exam is designed to evaluate the knowledge and skills of prospective secondary school science teachers to determine whether the candidate is at a sufficient level to be a beginning teacher. Individuals taking the test are usually beginning teachers, or those who have either recently decided to seek a particular license or certification, or who have moved to a state where the test is required or preferred.

Test Administration

The test is administered via computer through an international network of testing centers, including Prometric testing centers, some colleges and universities, as well as a variety of other locations. Although it is primarily used in the United States, the test is available at locations throughout the world. However, the test is not available at all times. Instead, there is a window of about two weeks per month during which the test may be taken. Test takers can opt to retake the test at any point as long as at least twenty-one days from the previous exam attempt have elapsed. Test takers should be prepared to show proper identification at the testing center. Test takers will also receive an orientation to the computer testing procedure upon admission to the testing center.

Accommodations for test takers meeting the requirements of the Americans with Disabilities Act include extended testing time, additional rest breaks, a separate testing room, a writer/recorder for answers, and a test reader. Tests in sign language, Braille, audio, or large print can also be requested for certain qualifying disabilities.

Test Format

The test addresses a wide range of science topics, including chemistry, physics, life science, and earth and space science. Within each topic, questions incorporate the understanding of various concepts, methods, terms, and problem-solving techniques. There are also questions that are not specific to a certain scientific field or topic, but that cover scientific methods and techniques applicable across the sciences. Question difficulty is roughly equivalent to a typical introductory college course, but some questions are purposely designed to be at a more advanced level to ensure that the prospective teacher has a deeper understanding of the sciences than his or her future students. In total, the test is comprised of 135 selected-response questions in which the test taker chooses from multiple-choice options or chooses a particular word, sentence, or part of a graphic. The approximate breakdown of the questions by subject area is as follows:

Content Category	# of Questions	Percentage of Exam
Scientific Methodology, Techniques, and History	15	11%
Physical Science	51	38%
Life Science	27	20%
Earth and Space Science	27	20%
Science, Technology, and Society	15	11%

Scoring

Raw scores are based on the number of correct responses; each correct answer is worth one raw point Test takers are not penalized for incorrect answers or guesses. The raw score is then converted to a scaled score, which ranges from 100 to 200. The scaling process is intended to ensure that scores obtained by test takers who receive different versions of the test are comparable to each other. The required passing score varies from state to state, from a low of 143 in South Dakota to a high of 166 in Utah.

ETS also offers a "Recognition of Excellence" to test takers who perform exceptionally well on the exam. The award is typically earned by those whose scores fall in the top fifteen percent of scores on the exam; in 2015, the required a score for this designation was 185.

Scientific Methodology, Techniques, and History

Methods of Scientific Inquiry and Design

Identifying Problems Based on Observations

Human beings are, by nature, very curious. Long before the scientific method was established, people have been making observations and predicting outcomes, manipulating the physical world to create extraordinary things—from the first man-made fire in 6000 B.C.E. to the satellite that orbited Pluto in 2016. Although the history of the scientific method is sporadic and attributed to many different people, it remains the most reliable way to obtain and utilize knowledge about the observable universe. The scientific method consists of the following steps:

- Make an observation
- Create a question
- Form a hypothesis
- Conduct an experiment
- Collect and analyze data
- Form a conclusion

The first step is to identify a problem based on an observation—the who, what, when, where, why, and how. An *observation* is the analysis of information using basic human senses: sight, sound, touch, taste, and smell. Observations can be two different types—qualitative or quantitative. A *qualitative observation* describes what is being observed, such as the color of a house or the smell of a flower. *Quantitative observations* measure what is being observed, such as the number of windows on a house or the intensity of a flower's smell on a scale of 1-5.

Observations lead to the identification of a problem, also called an *inference.* For example, if a fire truck is barreling down a busy street, the inferences could be:

- There's a fire.
- Someone is hurt.
- Some kid pulled the fire alarm at a local school.

Inferences are logical predictions based on experience or education that lead to the formation of a hypothesis.

Forming and Testing a Hypothesis

A *hypothesis* is a testable explanation of an observed scenario and is presented in the form of a statement. It's an attempt to answer a question based on an observation, and it allows a scientist to predict an outcome. A hypothesis makes assumptions on the relationship between two different variables, and answers the question: "If I do this, what happens to that?"

In order to form a hypothesis, there must be an independent variable and a dependent variable that can be measured. The *independent variable* is the variable that is manipulated, and the *dependent variable* is the result of the change.

For example, suppose a student wants to know how light affects plant growth. Based upon what he or she already knows, the student proposes (hypothesizes) that the more light to which a plant is exposed, the faster it will grow.

- Observation: Plants exposed to lots of light seem to grow taller.
- Question: Will plants grow faster if there's more light available?
- Hypothesis: The more light the plant has, the faster it will grow.
- Independent variable: The amount of time exposed to light (able to be manipulated)
- Dependent variable: Plant growth (the result of the manipulation)

Once a hypothesis has been formed, it must be tested to determine whether it's true or false. (How to test a hypothesis is described in a subsequent section.) After it has been tested and validated as true over and over, then a hypothesis can develop into a theory, model, or law.

Development of Theories, Models, and Laws

Theories, models, and laws have one thing in common: *they develop on the basis of scientific evidence that has been tested and verified by multiple researchers on many different occasions*. Listed below are their exact definitions:

- *Theory*: An explanation of natural patterns or occurrences—i.e., the theory of relativity, the kinetic theory of gases, etc.

- *Model:* A representation of a natural pattern or occurrence that's difficult or impossible to experience directly, usually in the form of a picture or 3-D representation—i.e., Bohr's atomic model, the double-helix model of DNA, etc.

- *Law:* A mathematical or concise description of a pattern or occurrence in the observable universe—i.e., Newton's law of gravity, the laws of thermodynamics, etc.

The terms *theory, model,* and *law* are often used interchangeably in the sciences, although there's an essential difference: theories and models are used to explain *how and why* something happens, while laws describe exactly *what* happens. A common misconception is that theories develop into laws. But theories and models never become laws because they inherently describe different things.

Type	Function	Examples
Theory	To explain how and why something happens	Einstein's Theory of Special Relativity The Big Bang Theory
Model	To represent how and why something happens	A graphical model or drawing of an atom
Laws	To describe exactly what happens	$E = mc^2$ $F = ma$ $PV = nRT$

In order to ensure that scientific theories are consistent, scientists continually gather information and evidence on existing theories to improve their accuracy.

Experimental Design

To test a hypothesis, one must conduct a carefully designed experiment. There are four basic requirements that must be present for an experiment to be valid:

1. A control
2. Variables
3. A constant
4. Repeated and collected data

The *control* is a standard to which the resultant findings are compared. It's the baseline measurement that allows for scientists to determine whether the results are positive or negative. For the example of light affecting plant growth, the control may be a plant that receives no light at all.

The *independent variable* is manipulated (a good way to remember this is *I* manipulate the *I*ndependent variable), and the *dependent variable* is the result of changes to the independent variable. In the plant example, the independent variable is the amount of time exposed to light, and the dependent variable is the resulting growth (or lack thereof) of the plant. For this experiment, there may be three plants—one that receives a minimal amount of light, the control, and one that receives a lot of light.

Finally, there must be constants in an experiment. A *constant* is an element of the experiment that remains unchanged. Constants are extremely important in minimizing inconsistencies within the experiment that may lead to results outside the parameters of the hypothesis. For example, some constants in the above case are that all plants receive the same amount of water, all plants are potted in the same kind of soil, the species of the plant used in each condition is the same, and the plants are stored at the same temperature. If, for instance, the plants received different amounts of water as well as light, it would be impossible to tell whether the plants responded to changes in water or light.

Once the experiment begins, a disciplined scientist must always record the observations in meticulous detail, usually in a journal. A good journal includes dates, times, and exact values of both variables and constants. Upon reading this journal, a different scientist should be able to clearly understand the experiment and recreate it exactly. The journal includes all *collected data*, or any observed changes. In this case, the data is rates of plant growth, as well as any other phenomena that occurred as a result of the experiment. A well-designed experiment also includes repetition in order to get the most accurate possible readings and to account for any errors, so several trials may be conducted.

Even in the presence of diligent constants, there are an infinite number of reasons that an experiment can (and will) go wrong, known as *sources of error*. All experimental results are inherently accepted as imperfect, if ever so slightly, because experiments are conducted by human beings, and no instrument can measure anything perfectly. The goal of scientists is to minimize those errors to the best of their ability. (Determining sources of error will be discussed in a subsequent section.)

Process Skills Including Observing, Comparing, Inferring, Categorizing, Generalizing, and Concluding

The skills needed to think critically, scientifically, and to follow the scientific method are referred to as *process skills*. These skills are the soil from which scientific knowledge is nurtured and grown. There are six fundamental process skills:

- *Observation*—using the senses to gather information

- *Communication*—using words, drawings, graphs, charts, or videos to effectively present observations

- *Classification*—grouping or categorizing objects or events based on certain attributes or criteria, i.e., sorting subjects into height and weight, grouping plants by species, etc.

- *Measurement*—using tools and instruments to describe dimensional variations in an object or event, such as measuring tape, graduated cylinders, clocks, etc.

- *Inference*—drawing conclusions from observations based on prior knowledge or education, i.e., "the grass is wet; it must have rained last night."

- *Prediction*—anticipating the outcome of an event based on prior knowledge or experiences, i.e., "there are many clouds in the sky; it's going to rain tonight." Prediction is the essential skill in forming a solid hypothesis.

In addition to the basic process skills, there are other skills needed in scientific experiments. One essential skill is *generalization*—a type of inference deduced by broad observations of large groups of people or objects that is used frequently in quantitative research. Because of the near-impossibility of sampling a whole population, generalizations are applied to represent a whole population as accurately as possible.

The final step of the scientific method is to make inferences from observed data, which is also known as forming a *conclusion*. Conclusions are placed at the end of scientific papers and wrap up the experimental procedure with its respective inferences. For example, if the experimental data from the plant growth experiment showed that plants with more light grew 2cm more than plants with minimal light in a given period of time, the conclusion may be that certain components of light stimulate plant growth, so the more light that a plant receives, the taller it will grow.

Nature of Scientific Knowledge

Subject to Change
The nature of science is to continuously gather knowledge in order to develop an understanding of the universe. Because of its experimental nature, there's no such thing as "absolute truth" in science. Even the oldest theories are constantly tested in order to improve our understanding or disregard those that no longer apply in light of new observations and interpretations.

Consistent with Evidence
Science is subject to change because of evidence presented in light of new findings. Science is dependent upon the inferences made from evidence obtained through observation. Introductions, expansions, and revisions of scientific theories must present evidence to ascertain that they're still true.

<u>Based on Reproducible Evidence</u>
Before scientific knowledge is established as true, it must be reproducible—that is, the entire experiment must be able to be duplicated by either the same scientist or a different one to ensure its validity.

<u>Includes Unifying Concepts and Processes</u>
Scientific knowledge must be unified, meaning there are central ideas common to all sciences from which new and improved information can grow. There are standards for unifying concepts and processes that students are required to learn in grades K-12, which include:

- Systems, Order, and Organization

    o Observing the universe in distinct parts and understanding all elements that compose these parts to form the whole—i.e., organisms, galaxies, cells, numbers, government, the entire known universe, etc.

- Evidence, Models, and Explanation

    o Scientific theories are based on collected evidence, which provides explanations and the basis for models that enhance understanding and enable scientists to make predictions.

- Change, Consistency, and Measurement

    o The natural world is consistently changing, yet many patterns are repeated over time—i.e., change of seasons, tidal phases, moon phases, etc.

- Evolution and Equilibrium

    o Organisms are genetically diverse, and traits that are advantageous for survival are passed on through the generations. Natural systems all trend towards equilibrium—a state of balance between opposing processes.

- Form and Function

    o There is a relationship between an object's structure and its function—i.e., tooth shape, cell shape, leaf thickness, etc.

Processes Involved in Scientific Data Collection and Manipulation

Common Units of Measurement

There are two primary systems of measurement: the metric system and the English system. The metric system is a system of decimals, and the English system is composed of arbitrary measurements.

<u>The Metric System</u>
The Metric System was developed in France during the French Revolution in 1799, in order to distinguish itself from the British Empire and also to create a universal system of measurement. Almost every country, except three, has adopted it as their official measuring system. The physical quantities of the

metric system are length, mass, volume, and time, and each has a basic unit of measurement: the meter (m), the gram (g), the liter (L), and the second (s), respectively.

Physical Quantity	Basic Unit of Measurement	Symbol
Length	meter	M
Mass	gram	G
Volume	liter	L
Time	second	S

Conversions within these measurements are easily made by multiplying or dividing by factors of ten and are indicated by the prefix attached to the unit. The most common units are listed below:

Prefix	Symbol	Factor	Power	Examples
kilo-	K	1,000	10^3	kilometer, kilogram, kiloliter, kilosecond
hecto-	H	100	10^2	hectometer, hectogram, hectoliter, hectosecond
deca-	Da	10	10^1	decameter, decagram, decaliter, decasecond
None	None	1	10^0	meter, gram, liter, second
deci-	D	0.1	10^{-1}	decimeter, decigram, deciliter, decisecond
centi-	C	0.01	10^{-2}	centimeter, centigram, centimeter, centisecond
milli-	M	0.001	10^{-3}	millimeter, milligram, milliliter, millisecond

Conversions within the Metric System
The wonderful thing about the metric system is it's incredibly easy to convert within the same unit of measurement—simply multiply or divide by ten!

Suppose a scientist wants to convert 23 meters to kilometers. The first method is to simply move the decimal point to the right or left depending on the prefix.

LEFT   RIGHT

kilo-   hecto-   deca-   UNIT   deci-   centi-   milli-

3   2   1   1   2   3

A decimal point for whole numbers always follows the ones unit—in this case, after the 3. To remember where the decimal is placed, imagine the number instead as 23.0.

After the decimal has been located, move it in accordance with the prefix. As shown above, *kilo* is *three* places to the *left* of the unit (meters, in this case). Therefore, the decimal is moved three units to the left:

$$23.0m \rightarrow {}_{\underset{3\ 2\ 1}{0230}} \rightarrow 0.023km$$

Thus, 23 meters is equivalent to 0.023 kilometers.

Another method of conversion relies on forming an equation. To demonstrate, one should follow the steps below:

1. Write down the problem.

$$23m = ?\, km$$

2. Identify the conversion.

$$1km = 1,000m$$

3. Write down the conversion as a fraction.

$$\frac{1km}{1,000m}$$

4. Write the original unit and conversion fraction as a multiplication problem.

$$23m \times \frac{1km}{1,000m}$$

5. Cancel units that appear on the top and bottom.

$$23\cancel{m} \times \frac{1km}{1,000\cancel{m}}$$

6. Solve the equation.

$$23\,m \times \frac{1km}{1,000\,m} = 0.023km$$

Again, 23 meters is equivalent to 0.023 kilometers.

The English System

The English system of measurement was developed centuries ago using the human body as well as familiar objects. The inch, for example, was the distance between King Henry I's second and third knuckle, and the foot was distance between his heel and toes. The common units of the English system are listed below:

Length	Mass	Volume
1 foot (ft.) = 12 inches (in)	16 ounces (oz.) = 1 pound (lb.)	16 fluid oz. (fly oz.) = 1 pint
3 feet (ft.) = 1 yard (yd.)	2,000 pounds (lb.) = 1 ton	2 pints = 1 quart
5,280 feet (ft.) = 1 mile (mi)		4 quarts = 1 gallon

Conversion within the English System

Due to the arbitrary nature of the English system, one cannot simply convert one unit to another by moving decimals. The best way to convert is to use the second method—equations—listed above.

Say, for example, a scientist wanted to convert 3.6 miles into feet. The second method for this problem could be condensed into the following:

$$3.6\,mi \times \frac{5,280ft}{1\,mi} = 19,008ft$$

Conversions Between Systems

Converting units between systems can be tricky because they follow different rules. The best way is to look up an English to Metric system conversion factor and then use the second method to solve the problem. The below table lists the common conversion values:

English System	Metric System
1 inch	2.54 cm
1 foot	0.3048 m
1 yard	0.914 m
1 mile	1.609 km
1 ounce	28.35 g
1 pound	0.454 kg
1 fluid ounce	29.574 mL
1 quart	0.946 L
1 gallon	3.785 L

Suppose a scientist wanted to convert 3.6 miles to meters. The second method for this problem could be condensed into the following:

$$3.6\,mi \times \frac{1.609\,km}{1\,mi} \times \frac{1,000\,m}{1\,km} = 5,792m$$

Scientific Notation and Significant Figures in Collected Data

Scientific Notation

Scientific notation is the conversion of extremely small or large numbers into a format that is easier to comprehend and manipulate. It changes the number into a product of two separate numbers: a digit term and an exponential term.

Scientific notation = digit term x exponential term

To put a number into scientific notation, one should use the following steps:

- Move the decimal point to after the first non-zero number to find the digit number.
- Count how many places the decimal point was moved in step 1.
- Determine if the exponent is positive or negative.
- Create an exponential term using the information from steps 2 and 3.
- Combine the digit term and exponential term to get scientific notation.

For example, to put 0.0000098 into scientific notation, the decimal should be moved so that it lies between the last two numbers: 000009.8. This creates the digit number:

9.8

Next, the number of places that the decimal point moved is determined; to get between the 9 and the 8, the decimal was moved six places to the right. It may be helpful to remember that a decimal moved to the right creates a negative exponent, and a decimal moved to the left creates a positive exponent. Because the decimal was moved six places to the right, the exponent is negative.

Now, the exponential term can be created by using the base 10 (this is *always* the base in scientific notation) and the number of places moved as the exponent, in this case:

10^{-6}

Finally, the digit term and the exponential term can be combined as a product. Therefore, the scientific notation for the number 0.0000098 is:

9.8 x 10^{-6}

Significant Figures

Significant figures are numbers that contribute meaning to a measurement. Reporting values in significant figures reduces unnecessary numbers while increasing accuracy and minimizing confusion. For example, if a scale measures a sample to four significant figures, say, 12.56 grams, it would be inaccurate to write the number as 12.5600, because it very well may be more or less than 12.5600, but the scale cannot provide the measurement to that degree of precision. Therefore, all data must be presented with the number of figures that accurately reflect the precision of the measuring instrument.

There are rules for identifying the number of significant figures in a number:

- All non-zero digits are significant.

  For example, the number 23 has two significant figures, and the number 165.74 has five significant figures.

- Any zeros between two non-zero numbers are significant.

  For example, the number 203 has three significant figures: 2, 0, and 3.

- Leading zeros are never significant.

  For example, the value 0.000034 has two significant figures: 3 and 4.

- Trailing zeros (those following a non-zero number) are only significant after a decimal point.

  For example, the value 0.034500 has five significant figures: 3, 4, 5, 0, and 0.

- In numbers without decimals, trailing zeros may or may not be significant.

  For example, a number like 1,600 may have two or four significant figures, depending if the number is precise to the nearest unit (four) or if it's just an estimate (two).

Scientific notation is often used to reduce numbers to significant figures. In scientific notation, the exponent doesn't count as a significant figure. For example, to reduce the number 0.0000098 (which has two significant figures) into a number that only has significant figures, it can be written in scientific notation 9.8×10^{-6}, where the 9 and the 8 are the only significant numbers. It's important to notice here that the number of significant figures remains the same, but one has an unnecessary number of zeros, and the other has none.

Organizing and Presenting Data

Observations made during a scientific experiment are organized and presented as data. Data can be collected in a variety of ways, depending on the purpose of the experiment. In testing how light exposure affects plant growth, for example, the data collected would be changes in the height of the plant relative to the amount of light it received. The easiest way to organize collected data is to use a *data table*.

A data table always contains a title that relates the two variables in the experiment. Each column or row must contain the units of measurement in the heading only. See the below example (note: this is not actual data).

Plant Growth During Time Exposed to Light (130 Watts)	
Time (Hours)	Height (cm)
0	3.2
192	5.0
480	7.9
720	12.1

Data must be presented in a concise, coherent way. Most data is presented in graph form. The fundamental rule for creating a graph based on data is that the independent variable (i.e., amount of time exposed to light) is on the x-axis, and the dependent variable (i.e., height of plant) is on the y-axis.

There are many types of graphs that a person may choose to use depending on which best represents the data.

A *bar graph* is used when counting or categorizing data. For example, the number of commuters who travel via four different modes of transportation.

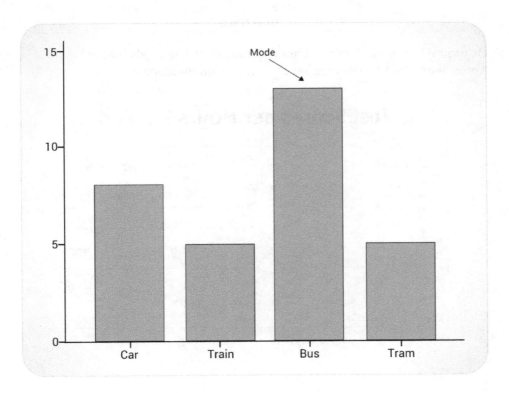

A *line graph* is used when there are changes in the dependent variable ranging from low to high, or when collecting data over a period of time. This graph would be the best to use for the plant growth experiment.

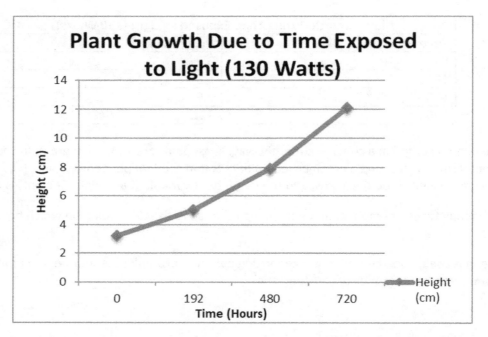

A *scatter plot* is used when more than one data point exists on the y-axis for each value of the x-axis, such as test scores dependent on the number of hours a student studied.

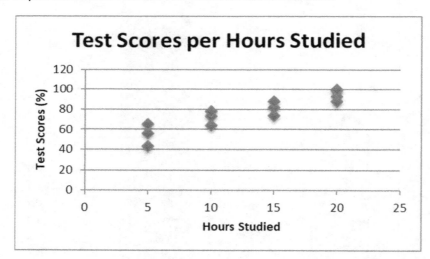

A *pie* or *circle graph* is used when the data sum to 100%, such as the percentage of students in each high school class interested in a trip to a local museum.

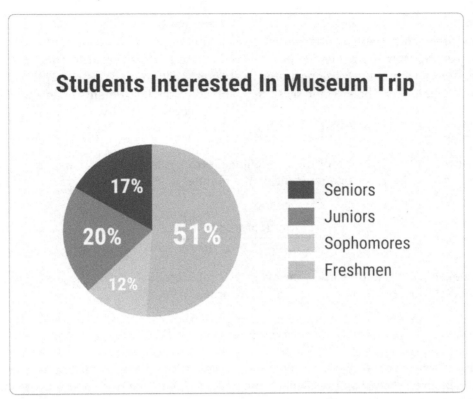

Students Interested In Museum Trip

17%

20%   51%

12%

- Seniors
- Juniors
- Sophomores
- Freshmen

Basic Data and Error Analysis

For a hypothesis to be proven true or false, all experiments are subject to multiple trials in order to verify accuracy and precision. A measurement is *accurate* if the observed value is close to the "true value." For example, if someone measured the pH of water at 6.9, this measurement would be considered accurate (the pH of water is 7). On the other hand, a measurement is *precise* if the measurements are consistent—that is, if they are reproducible. If someone had a series of values for a pH of water that were 6.9, 7.0, 7.2, and 7.3, their measurements would not be precise. However, if all measured values were 6.9, or the average of these values was 6.9 with a small range, then their measurements would be precise. Measurements can fall into the following categories:

- Both accurate and precise
- Accurate but not precise
- Precise but not accurate
- Neither accurate nor precise

The accuracy and precision of observed values most frequently correspond to the amount of error present in the experiment. Aside from general carelessness, there are two primary types of error: random and systematic. *Random errors* are unpredictable variations in the experiment that occur by chance. They can be difficult to detect, but they can often be nullified using a statistical analysis and minimized by taking repeated measurements and taking an average. *Systematic errors* occur when there are imperfections in the design of the experiment itself—usually errors that affect the accuracy of the measurements. These errors can be minimized by using the most accurate equipment available and by taking proper care of instruments and measuring techniques. Common examples of error are listed below.

Random	Systematic
Environmental factors (random changes in vibration, temperature, humidity, etc.)	Poorly maintained instruments
	Old or out-of-date instruments
Differences in instrument use among scientists	Faulty calibration of instruments
Errors in judgment—can be affected by state of mind	Reading the instruments at an angle (parallax error) or other faulty reading errors
Incorrectly recorded observations	Not accounting for lag time

The most basic method to account for the possibility of errors is to take an average (also called a *mean*) of all observed values. To do so, one must divide the number of measurements taken from the sum of all measurements.

$$\frac{Sum\ of\ Measurements}{Total\ \#\ of\ Measurements}$$

For the above example of the pH values, the average is calculated by finding the sum of the pH values ascertained and dividing by the number of values recorded.

$$\frac{6.9 + 7.0 + 7.2 + 7.3}{4} = 7.1$$

The more observations recorded, the greater the precision. It's important to first assess the accuracy of measurements before proceeding to collect multiple trials of data. If a particular trial results in measurements that are vastly different from the average, it may indicate that a random or systematic error occurred during the trial. When this happens, a scientist might decide to "throw out" the trial and run the experiment again.

Interpreting and Drawing Conclusions from Data Presented in Tables, Graphs, Maps, and Charts

Trends in Data

The ability to recognize trends in data allows scientists to make predictions, not only about the present or near future (such as in a hypothesis), but also about the distant future and even the past. The practice of collecting data and spotting patterns is referred to as *trend analysis*.

Graphs, charts, and tables are helpful in interpreting quantitative data because they provide a visual representation that can be easily analyzed. Graphs are typically created from the tables and charts in which the data were collected. The line graph on plant growth, for example, was created from the data table of observations. The methods in which data are presented (graphs, charts, etc.) are simply ways for scientists to determine trends by recognizing relationships between variables.

Relationships Between Variables

The most common relationship examined in an experiment is between two variables (independent and dependent), most often referred to as *x* and *y*. The independent variable (*x*) is displayed on the horizontal axis of a coordinate plane, and the dependent variable (*y*) is displayed on the vertical axis.

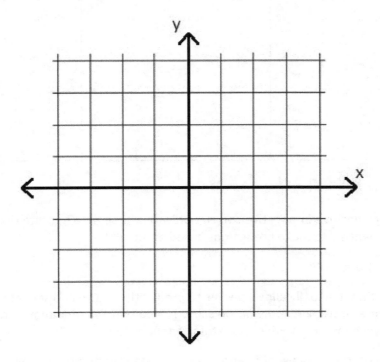

The placement of the variables in this way provides a visual representation of what happens to *y* when *x* is manipulated. In analyzing trends, *x* is used to predict *y*, and since *y* is the result of *x*, then *x* comes before *y* in time. For example, in the experiment on plant growth, the hours the plant was exposed to light had to happen before growth could occur.

When analyzing the relationship between the variables, scientists will consider the following questions:

- Does *y* increase or decrease with *x*, or does it do both?

- If it increases or decreases, how fast does it change?

- Does *y* stay steady through certain values of *x*, or does it jump dramatically from one value to the other?

- Is there a strong relationship? If given a value of *x*, can one predict what will happen to *y*?

If, in general, *y* increases as *x* increases, or *y* decreases and *x* decreases, it is known as a *positive correlation*. The data from the plant experiment show a positive correlation—as time exposed to light (*x*) increases, plant growth (*y*) increases. If the variables trend in the opposite direction of each other—that is, if *y* increases as *x* decreases, or vice versa—it is called a *negative correlation*. If there doesn't seem to be any visible pattern to the relationship, it is referred to as *no* or *zero correlation*.

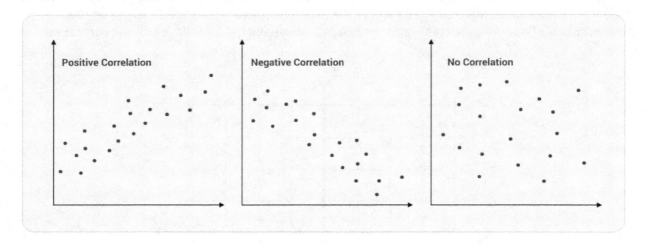

Experiments that show positive or negative correlation within their data indicate that the variables are related. This allows scientists to make predictions based on the data.

Predictions Based on Data

Science is amazing in that it actually allows people to predict the future and see into the past with a certain degree of accuracy. Using numerical correlations created from quantitative data, one can see in a general way what will happen to *y* when something happens to *x*.

The best way to get a useful overview of quantitative data to facilitate predictions is to use a scatter plot, which plots each data point individually. As shown above, there may be slight fluctuations from the correlation line, so one may not be able to predict what happens with *every* change, but he or she will be able to have a general idea of what is going to happen to *y* with a change in *x*. To demonstrate, the graph with a line of best fit created from the plant growth experiment is below.

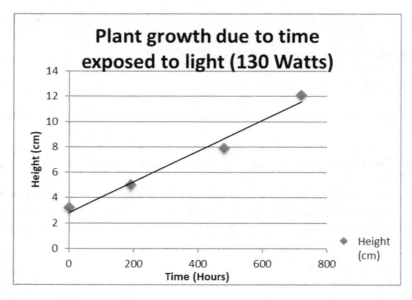

Using the trend line within the data, one can estimate what will happen to plant growth at a given length of time exposed to light. For example, it can be estimated that with 700 hours of time, the plant is expected to grow to a height of about 11 cm. The plant may not grow to exactly 11 cm, but it will likely grow to about that height based on previous data. This process allows scientists to draw conclusions based on data.

Drawing Valid Conclusions Based on Data

Drawing conclusions is the process of analyzing patterns in data and determining whether the relationship is *causal*, meaning that one variable is the cause of the change in the other. There are many correlations that aren't casual, such as a city where alcohol sales increase as crime increases. Although there's a positive correlation between the two, crime may not be the factor that causes an increase in alcohol sales. There could be other factors, such as an increase in unemployment, which increases both alcohol sales and crime rates. Although crime and alcohol sales are positively correlated, they aren't causally correlated.

For this reason, it's important for scientists to carefully design their experiments with all the appropriate constants to ensure that the relationships are causal. If a relationship is determined to be causal by isolating the variables from all other factors, only then can conclusions be drawn based on data. In the plant growth experiment, the conclusion is that light affects plant growth, because the data shows they are causally correlated since the two variables were entirely isolated.

Procedures for Correct Preparation, Storage, Use, and Disposal of Laboratory Materials

Appropriate and Safe Use of Materials

The appropriate and safe use of laboratory materials not only reduces the potential harm to people and the environment, but also minimizes waste and ensures accurate data collection. The following guidelines highlight the crucial skills in safely handling chemical reagents and specimens.

Identifying Hazards
The ability to identify a hazard allows one to take safety measures such as wearing the appropriate clothing and respond appropriately to spills.

Identifying Hazards

Common types of laboratory hazards include:

- Chemical hazards
- Toxins
- Corrosives
- Flammables
- Reactive substances
- Biological hazards
- Animals
- Plants
- Microbes
- Genetically-modified organisms
- Physical hazards
- Extreme heat
- Extreme cold
- Noise
- Heating devices
- Projectiles
- Electrical hazards

- Fire
- Shock
- Radiation hazards
- Ionizing radiation
- Non-iodizing radiation
- Mechanical hazards
- Machinery
- Airborne hazards
- Vapor
- Fume
- Dust

Handling Chemicals and Specimens

A *specimen* is any substance or fluid taken from a plant, animal, or other object, such as urine, blood, saliva, stool, or tissue. To safely handle chemicals and specimens, one should adhere to the following guidelines:

- Always read the safety data sheet that accompanies a chemical.
- Make sure specimens and chemicals are properly stored.
- Ensure that any first-aid equipment, including eye-washing stations, are close and ready for use.
- Keep all work stations clean and sanitized.
- Use the smallest amount of chemical or specimen possible.
- Make sure all containers are properly labeled.
- Use substitutions for more harmful chemicals whenever possible.

Safe Disposal of Materials

The following are basic requirements to follow for the disposal of chemical hazardous waste:

Create a Hazardous Waste Area

- Select an area near the source of the waste, out of the way of normal lab activities, and easily accessible to all lab personnel.

- Label the area "Danger—Hazardous Waste" with the following sign:

<u>Deposit Chemicals into the Appropriate Containers</u>

- Make sure that containers into which the chemicals will be discarded are stable enough to hold them—chemicals must not weaken or dissolve the material of the container.

- Acids and bases cannot be stored with metal
- Hydrofluoric acid cannot be stored with glass.
- Solvents (i.e. gasoline) cannot be stored in polyethylene containers, such as a milk jug.

- Waste containers must come with lids and caps that are resistant to leakage, and containers should be closed at all times, except when opened to add more waste.

- The size of the container should be appropriate for the amount of expected waste.

- Waste containers should be placed inside a larger, empty container to catch any waste that may potentially spill or leak.

Attach a Hazardous Waste Tag
Complete and attach the following hazardous waste tag to all containers:

Hazardous Waste Tag

Front

HAZARDOUS WASTE
FEDERAL LAW PROHIBITS IMPROPER DISPOSAL

IF FOUND, CONTACT THE NEAREST POLICE OR PUBLIC SAFETY
AUTHORITY OR THE U.S. ENVIRONMENT PROTECTION AGENCY.

PROPER D.O.T.
SHIPPING NAME _____ UN OR NA _____

GENERATOR INFORMATION:

NAME _____ ADDRESS _____

CITY _____ STATE _____ ZIP _____

EPA I.D. NO. _____ MANIFEST DOCUMENT NO. _____

EPA WASTE NO. _____ ACCUMULATION START DATE _____

HANDLE WITH CARE!
CONTAINS HAZARDOUS OR TOXIC WASTES

Back

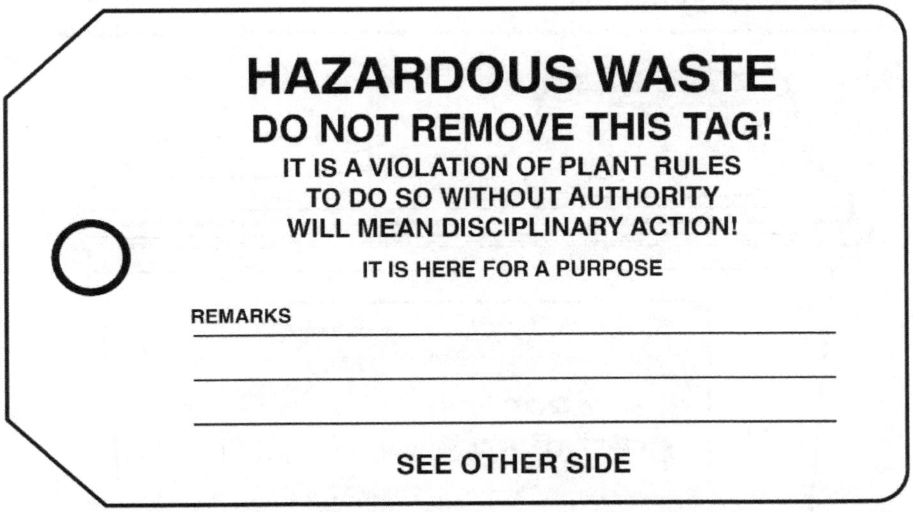

HAZARDOUS WASTE
DO NOT REMOVE THIS TAG!
IT IS A VIOLATION OF PLANT RULES
TO DO SO WITHOUT AUTHORITY
WILL MEAN DISCIPLINARY ACTION!

IT IS HERE FOR A PURPOSE

REMARKS _____

_____

_____

SEE OTHER SIDE

Requirements for Liquid Waste
- Don't overfill containers—be sure to leave at least 10% space between the container opening and the surface of the waste.

- Never mix liquid and solid waste.

- Double-bag small containers, such as vials, in clear plastic bags.

- Bag small containers composed of the same kind of waste.

- Attach a completed hazardous waste tag to all bags and containers.

Requirements for Solid Waste
Chemical solid waste is composed of three different categories: lab trash, dry chemicals, and sharps.

- Lab trash
- Use for waste such as Kim Wipes, disposable gloves, paper towels, and wooden stirrers
- Double-bag in clear bags
- Attach a completed hazardous waste tag to all bags
- Dry chemicals
- Return the chemical waste to the original container in which it was purchased.
- Attach a completed hazardous waste tag.
- Sharps

  - Examples include glass (broken or intact), pipettes and pipette tips, needles, X-ACTO™ knives, or anything capable of piercing, cutting, slicing, or tearing human flesh.

- Discard any used sharps into a designated sharps container with a biohazard sign.

Biohazard container

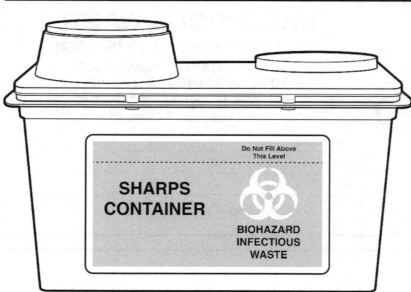

Appropriate Storage

Proper chemical storage is imperative for laboratory operations as well as the safety of all lab personnel. The following is a list of guidelines for the appropriate storage of chemicals and other hazardous materials:

1. There must be a designated place for each type of chemical.

   o   Flammables and volatile poisons (poisons that easily evaporate at room temperature) must be stored in cabinets, refrigerators, or freezers marked with a flammable label.

   o   Oxidizing acids, organic and mineral acids, liquid bases, liquid oxidizers, and non-volatile liquid poisons must be stored in a safety cabinet.

   o   Oxidizing acids must be double-contained.

   o   Solids should be stored above liquids.

   o   As a rule of thumb, different compounds should be stored separately.

2. Chemicals should not be permanently stored in any fume hood.
3. All containers should be kept sealed unless in use.
4. All chemicals must be kept away from sunlight and heat.
5. All chemicals must be labeled properly.
6. No chemical, except for bleach and cleaning agents, should be stored under the sink.

Preparing Equipment for Classroom or Field Use

Conducting a science lab is one of the most exciting ways to teach science. It not only allows students to experience science as professionals do, but gives them the opportunity to apply learned concepts to real-world scenarios. Before beginning a lab, instructors should:

- Know and clarify the concepts and theories upon which the experiment is based

- Test the experiment and equipment, following along in the student instruction manual to identify any potential issues

The most common preparations a science instructor will conduct are preparing solutions, staining slides, and labeling samples.

<u>Preparing a Solution of a Given Concentration</u>
The primary way that a solution is measured is expressed in terms of *molarity*. A solution's molarity is the number of moles per liter of a pure substance.

$$\text{Molarity (M) = moles/L}$$

A *mole* is the mass of pure substance (including atoms and all corresponding chemical units, such as elements and particles) containing the same number of constituent units as there are atoms in exactly 12.000 grams of ^{12}C. It's equivalent to 6.022×10^{23} molecules, also known as Avogadro's Number.

Most solutions are made by using a pure solid or by diluting a stock solution.

<u>Using a Pure Solid</u>
Instructors should follow this procedure for making a solution from a pure solid:

1. Determine the molecular mass of the solid.
2. Calculate the mass needed to make the solution.
3. Weigh out the substance and place it in the appropriate flask.
4. Dissolve solute in less water than the desired volume.
5. Fill the flask to the desired amount of solution.

Because standard weighing devices cannot measure a compound in moles, one must determine the molecular mass of a substance, which is expressed in g/mol. The molecular mass of an element can be found in a periodic table.

For example, an experiment calls for 400 mL of a 0.750 M solution of NaOH. To determine the atomic weight of the formula, one must add each element's molecular mass together.

Total molecular weight (NaOH) = 22.990 g/mol + 15.999 g/mol + 1.0078 g/mol = *39.997 g/mol* (the reported molecular weights are in five significant figures).

Once the molecular weight has been determined, the mass needed to make 400 mL of a 0.750 M solution of NaOH can be calculated by multiplying the volume of the solution (400 mL) by the molarity (0.750 mol/L) and the molecular weight of the substance (39.007 g/mol).

By entering the values, the total grams needed are calculated as follows:

	Sodium	Oxygen	Hydrogen	
Total molecular weight (NaOH) =	Na^{11}	O^8	H^1	**= 39.997 g/mol**
	22.990	15.999	1.0078	

Volume needed   Molarity   Molecular weight

$$\text{mL of solution} \times \frac{\text{mol substance}}{\text{1000 mL solution}} \times \frac{\text{g of substance}}{\text{mol of substance}} = \text{grams of substance needed to make solution}$$

$$\text{400 mL NaOH solution} \times \frac{\text{0.750 mol NaOH}}{\text{1000 mL NaOH solution}} \times \frac{\text{39.997 g NaOH}}{\text{1 mol NaOH}} = \text{12.015 g NaOH}$$

Because the required solution is given with three significant figures, the weight in grams should be measured at three significant figures as well, so only 12.0 grams is necessary for this solution.

Finally, the experimenter will weigh 12.0 grams of NaOH and place it in a 500-mL volumetric flask. About 200 mL of distilled water can be added and mixed until the solute has dissolved. Then more water is added until the flask reads 400 mL.

Using a Stock Solution

Stock solutions are used frequently in labs, as many substances are considered too hazardous to have in their pure form. For example, an experiment calls for a 500 mL solution of 1.25 M of HCl (hydrochloric acid). To save space, a school's stockroom would likely have a bottle of 12.0 M HCl that would then be diluted with water to form the desired concentration. Instructors should follow the procedure below to create the desired solution using a stock:

- Calculate the appropriate volume of stock solution to add to water.
- Add the correct amount of stock to a flask containing some of the required water.
- Dilute with water until desired volume is reached.

To make a 500 mL solution of 1.25 M HCl from a 12.0 M stock of HCl, the appropriate ratio must be set up. Because the total amount of the solute doesn't change when water is added, the moles of solute from the stock solution equal the moles of solute in the dilute solution:

Moles of Solute in Stock Solution = Moles of Solute in Dilute Solution

To calculate the moles of solute, one must multiply the volume (V) of the solution times the molarity (M) of the solution: M x V.

M x V (stock) = M x V (dilute)

Or

$M_SV_S = M_DV_D$

$M_S = 12.0$ $V_S = ?$ $M_D = 1.25$ $V_D = 500$ mL

Using algebra, the necessary volume of stock solution can be solved:

$$V_S = \frac{M_DV_D}{M_S}$$

$$V_S(ml) = \frac{(1.25M)(500ml)}{12.0M} = 52.1ml$$

Finally, 52.1 mL of the stock solution can be measured into a volumetric flask containing 200 ml of water. More water should be added until the volume reads 500 mL, and presto! There's 500 mL of a 1.25 M HCl solution. It's important to note that when diluting stock acid solutions, the acid should always be added to the water instead of the reverse. This is to prevent the acid from splashing out of the container and damaging laboratory equipment or causing bodily harm.

Staining Slides

Microscope slides are the mounts that specimens are placed upon in order to observe them under a microscope. Specimens may be *dry mounted*, or placed directly between the slide and cover slip, or they may be *wet mounted*, in which the specimen is suspended in an aqueous solution between the slide and cover slip. Staining a slide requires a wet mount.

To stain a slide, an instructor should follow this procedure:

1. Obtain a clean slide and cover slip.

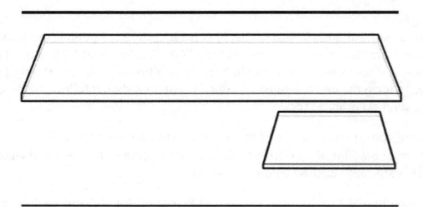

2. Place a *very thin* slice of the specimen directly in the middle of the slide.

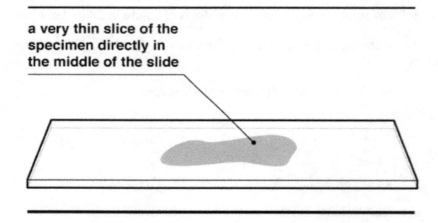

a very thin slice of the specimen directly in the middle of the slide

3. Add a drop of water to the specimen using a pipette.

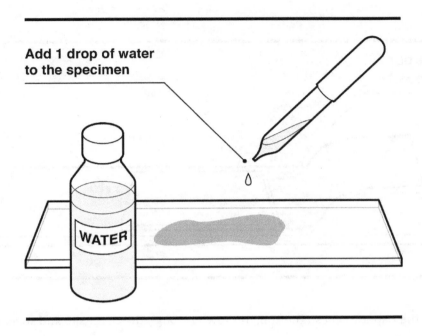

Add 1 drop of water to the specimen

WATER

4. Add the cover slip by placing the slip on its edge and lowering it onto the specimen from a 45° angle.

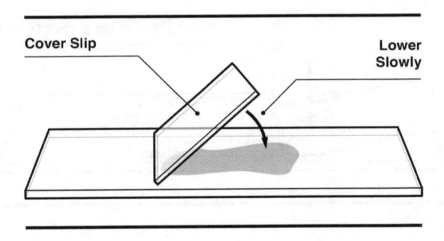

Cover Slip

Lower Slowly

5. Add the appropriate stain (table below) on one side of the cover slip and a piece of paper towel on the other side.

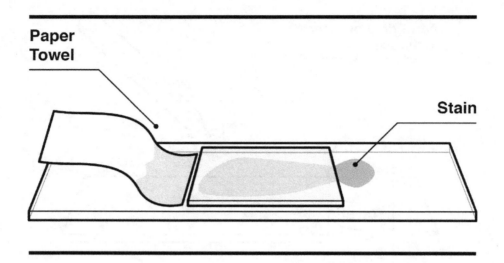

6. Press down on the paper towel so the stain is drawn through the cover slip and specimen.

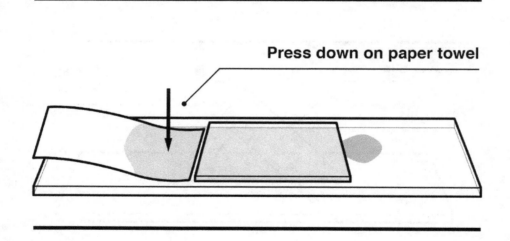

When choosing a stain, this table may be helpful:

Stain	Function	Uses
Eosin Y	Stains pink for alkaline cells (blood, cytoplasm, membranes)	Blood and bone marrow testing
Iodine	Stains brown or bluish-black for carbohydrates	Identify starches in plant and animal specimens
Gram's Stain	Stains purple for bacteria	Identify bacteria
Methylene Blue	Stains blue for acidic cells by allowing them to show against their background	Identifying acidic cell nucleic, DNA

Labeling Samples

All chemicals and collected specimens need appropriate labels to minimize confusion, which could have disastrous results. For samples within a laboratory, the following key information should be included:

- Name or initials of the researcher
- Date sample was prepared or collected
- Identification
- Chemical formula or name
- Identification number (if applicable)
- Any solvents or solutions that a sample is suspended in (such as water or acid)

How to Use Standard Equipment in the Laboratory and the Field

Appropriate and Safe Use

<u>Bunsen Burner</u>

Bunsen Burner

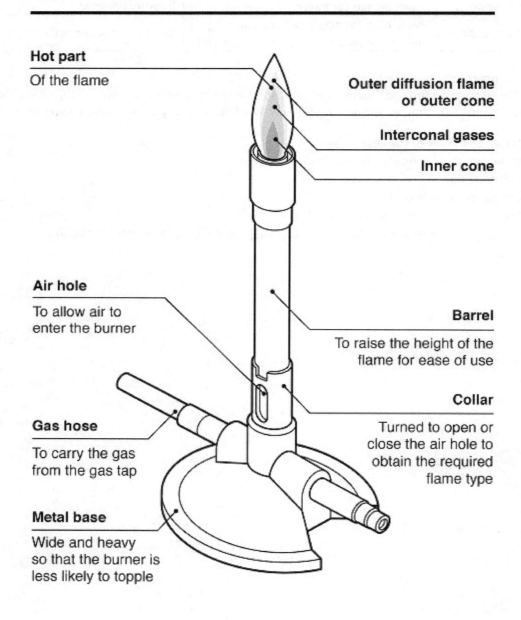

Hot part

Of the flame

Outer diffusion flame or outer cone

Interconal gases

Inner cone

Air hole

To allow air to enter the burner

Barrel

To raise the height of the flame for ease of use

Collar

Turned to open or close the air hole to obtain the required flame type

Gas hose

To carry the gas from the gas tap

Metal base

Wide and heavy so that the burner is less likely to topple

For the safe and appropriate use of a Bunsen burner, instructors and students should adhere to these guidelines:

Preparation

- Select a fireproof workstation (such as fireproof bench) and one near fire-extinguishing tools, such as a fire blanket or fire extinguisher.

- Be sure that the area beneath and around the burner is clean and free of flammable objects.

- Check all parts of the burner to ensure nothing is broken or damaged.

- Inspect the rubber gas hose for cracks and replace the hose if cracks are identified.

- Employ personal safety measures

- Wear safety goggles

- Wear tight-fitting clothing

- Tie back long hair

- Remove jewelry

- Attach the gas hose to the burner and the main gas valve, ensuring the hose is up far enough so that no gas can escape except through the hose.

- Turn the collar of the burner so that air holes are nearly closed. (This ensures that the ignition flame is relatively cool.)

Lighting

- Always handle the burner at the base
- Have the lighting tool ready, such as a match, a striker, or a long-barreled lighter
- Turn on the gas immediately before preparing to light
- Place the lighting device about 3-5 cm above the top of barrel
- Ensure the lighting device is within the gas stream
- Light the device and put out the match or lighter once the flame is going

Glassware
To properly select and handle glassware, one should follow these guidelines:

- Do the research—ensure that the glassware can hold the desired chemical reaction without breaking, corroding, or dissolving.

- Always inspect glassware before use and discard any glassware with cracks or chips in the designated container.

- Always use two hands when handling all glassware.

- Unless glassware is designed to do so, never heat or cool it.

- Always be aware that hot glass and cold glass look the same.

<u>Microscope</u>
There are two types of microscopes commonly used in a school lab: a compound microscope and a stereomicroscope. One must be sure to place microscopes on a flat, sturdy surface.

Compound Microscope
To use a compound microscope, one should follow these guidelines:

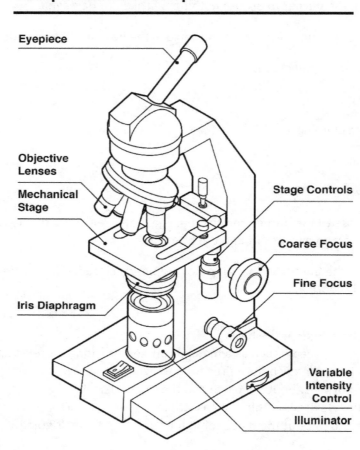

Compound Microscope

Eyepiece

Objective Lenses

Mechanical Stage

Iris Diaphragm

Stage Controls

Coarse Focus

Fine Focus

Variable Intensity Control

Illuminator

1. Place the microscope slide on the mechanical stage and secure it with the stage clips.

2. Move the objective lenses so that the lowest power is positioned over the stage.

3. Look through the eyepiece and turn the fine focus knob (which moves the stage upward) until the image comes into focus. If there's no image, move the slide around until the specimen comes into view.

4. Adjust the iris diaphragm and the variable intensity control to maximize the amount of light while still being able to see the specimen.

5. Once there's a clear image, turn the objective lens to a higher power setting. This may require adjustments of the iris diaphragm and intensity control to refocus the image.

6. Never let the objective lens touch the slide!

7. When finished, lower the stage, remove the slide, and power off the microscope.

Stereomicroscope
To use a stereomicroscope, one should follow these guidelines:

Stereomicroscope

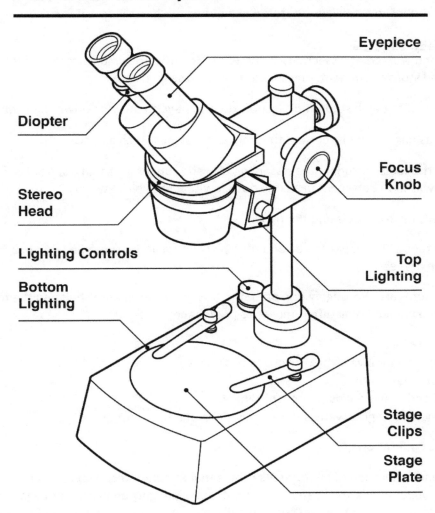

1. Place specimen on stage plate and secure with stage clips.

2. Switch on microscope lights. For microscope slides, use bottom lighting. For solid objects, use top lighting.

3. Look through the eyepiece and adjust the focus knob until the image comes into focus.

4. When finished, turn off the microscope and remove the specimen.

Appropriate Equipment Storage

Storage of pH Probes
Due to the sensitivity of the pH meter, it's imperative to store the probes in a buffer solution to ensure that the electrodes don't dry out. The kind of buffer solution depends on the pH meter, so it's essential to read the instruction manual that accompanies the pH meter to determine the kind of buffer solution to purchase. The probes must always be stored in a buffer solution when not in use.

Storage of Dissection Equipment
Proper cleaning and storage of dissection equipment is essential to avoid corrosion of the metal. To properly clean and store equipment, one should follow these guidelines:

- Include a wet rag with student dissection kits and have them wipe down their tools after use.

- Before washing any tools, be sure to remove any blades (such as a scalpel).

- Wash all the tools, including the dissecting tray and rubber insert, in a specialized laboratory (not dishwashing) detergent in a large bucket with a little bit of water.

- Thoroughly rinse all tools and the tray.

- Dry each tool with a paper towel, and then place them in the sun or in front of a fan to ensure maximum dryness.

- Once the tools are thoroughly dry, place the trays on a designated shelf and the tools in a large storage tub and add moisture remover to prevent corrosion.

Storage of Glassware
- Keep all glassware away from the edges of shelves.
- Never stack glassware.
- Use shelf and drawer pads to prevent sliding.
- Always ensure the glassware is thoroughly clean and dry before storage.

Maintenance and Calibration

Proper cleaning and calibration of instruments is essential to obtain the most accurate readings and also to help tools last longer. *Calibration* refers to the process of gauging an instrument against a certain standard to ensure accuracy of readings, such as calibrating a pH meter at 7.0. The following guidelines for the proper maintenance and calibration of certain instruments should be followed:

- Cleaning a microscope

    o Always clean microscopes with specialized lens-cleaning tissues.

    o Clean microscope lenses and eyepieces with an ammonia solution—one eyedropper full of ammonia in half a cup of water.

- If there are stubborn spots, rub them with isopropyl alcohol.
- Always keep microscopes covered in plastic or a specialized microscope cover.

- Calibrating a balance

  Almost all analytical balances—the kind used in the laboratory—come with an instruction manual on how to calibrate them. However, calibrating a balance is generally easy, and can be done by following these steps:

- Remove any debris from balancing plate

- Turn on the balance

- If balance reads anything other than 0.00, press the TARE button

- Balance should now read 0.00

Preparing the Classroom for Labs

Before teaching a lab or managing field research, it's essential for the instructor to be prepared.

Pre-Laboratory Setup
To prepare for a science lab, an instructor should:

1. Practice the lab before setting it up; this will help anticipate any kinks in the experiment, as well as determine the equipment needed at each lab station. It will also help set a foundation for any questions students may have regarding the instructions.

2. Determine the number of stations needed by analyzing the number of available tools and the number of students in the class. Be certain that every student has access to a sink, either individually or shared with other classmates.

3. Equip each station with only the tools necessary for that particular lab. Students may become distracted by extraneous tools.

4. Post rules for using the lab equipment, including proper use and cleanup, at each lab station.

Classroom Demonstrations
Before students to conduct a lab, a classroom demonstration can be a helpful visual aid. A demonstration should be done not only to show the proper execution of the lab protocol, but also to clarify the reasons for doing it and to hone in on essential concepts. They're also a fantastic way to get students engaged—more complicated experiments can be demonstrated by the instructor than those reasonably given to students, which can get students excited for the magic of participating in real science.

To prepare for a classroom demonstration, an instructor should practice, ideally with some honest friends. Friends can give feedback and point out anything that may be confusing. Demonstrations can take the form of PowerPoint® presentations, videos, or interactions with physical objects, such as the performance of an experiment.

<u>Field Research</u>

Field research is the collection and observation of information outside the laboratory. It can involve a wide range of activities and settings, from going into the forest to collect bark from different tree species, or conducting surveys on people in an experimental group. Field research in education usually consists of taking the students on a field trip. The type of field trip depends on the objective. To plan a smooth outing, it behooves the instructor to follow these steps:

1. Determine the objective of the field trip—how will this relate to the current field of study?

2. Select a site to visit depending on the objective. If, for example, an instructor wishes to instruct students on the reproduction of trees, he or she might take the students to a national forest. If the instructor wants the students to learn about careers in science, he or she may take them to a research facility or local university.

3. Call and arrange a visit with the facility, if necessary, and ask for any visitor information, such as a brochure.

4. Plan a schedule for the day, including transportation, arrival times, lunch times, a schedule of activities, and departure times. Visit the site before the trip and follow the schedule to work out any unforeseen issues, bringing any necessary equipment.

5. Discuss the purpose of the trip with the students and how it relates to the current topic of study, and go over the schedule.

6. Refer to the school's policies on how to obtain parental permission, transportation, and other field trip logistics.

Safety and Emergency Procedures in the Laboratory

Location and Use of Standard Safety Equipment

It's crucial that an instructor is familiar with the use and location of all available safety equipment before conducting a lab. The following list is an example of the primary forms of safety equipment that should be accessible in all scientific labs:

Chemical Fume Hood

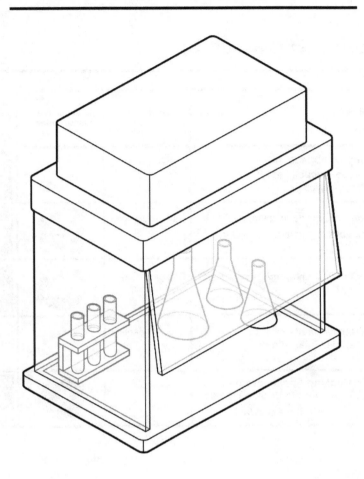

Fume hoods keep flammable fumes isolated within a fire-resistant enclosure, away from flames and toxic chemicals. It's advised to keep the mobile window (called the *sash*) closed when not in use, especially for particular toxic chemicals, and to not store too many chemicals in the hood, because this reduces its functionality. An annual inspection for all fume hoods must be scheduled to ensure proper function.

<u>Fire Extinguishers</u>

Fire extinguishers should be mounted on a wall and completely accessible with no obstructions. There are many different types of fire extinguishers and they are labeled by their class. The table below illustrates the different types of fire extinguishers:

Fire Extinguisher Classes

Class of Fire	Type of Fire	Type of Extinguisher	Extinguisher Identification	Symbol
A	**Ordinary combustibles** wood, paper, rubber, fabrics, and many plastics	Water, Dry Powder, Halon	A	
B	**Flammable Liquids and Gases** gasoline, oils, paint, lacquer, and tar	Carbon Dioxide, Dry Powder, Halon	B	
C	**Fires involving Live Electrical Equipment**	Carbon Dioxide, Dry Powder, Halon	C	
D	**Combustible Metals or Combustible Metal Alloys**	Special Agents	D	No Picture Symbol D
K	**Fires in Cooking Appliances that involve Combustible Cooking Media** vegetable or animal oils and fats		K	

Most extinguishers are ABC extinguishers, meaning they can put out class A, B, and C fires. It's essential to read the instructions and receive proper training in every classroom.

Fire extinguishers are only used when a fire is just getting going, and are useless against large fires. If the fire is taller than a person, instructors should evacuate all students. The basic steps for using an extinguisher are displayed below, and can be remembered using the acronym *PASS*:

- *P*ull the pin
- *A*im the nozzle at the base of the fire—not the top of the flames
- *S*queeze the trigger
- *S*weep the spray from side to side

Safety Shower

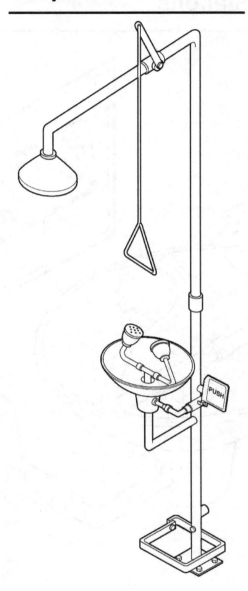

Safety showers are required wherever toxic chemicals are in use. They are generally activating by pulling down on a lever attached to a valve. In the event of chemical contamination on skin or clothing, follow these directions:

- Before conducting a lab, locate the shower's shut-off valve
- Remove any contaminated clothing
- Flush the body for at least 15 minutes before seeking medical attention

Eyewash Stations

Eyewashes are also essential for the initial treatment of chemical contamination. Before conducting a lab, show students the location of the eyewash.

If a chemical gets into the eyes, follow these directions:

- Get any injured personnel to the eyewash station as quickly as possible and remove contacts if they're in place.
- Turn on the valve and flush eyes for 15 minutes, using fingers to hold eyelids open.
- Call (or have someone else call) for medical attention while eyes are flushing.

Laboratory Safety Rules for Students

All instructors should have a written set of rules either posted on the wall where students can read them or given as a handout and signed by each student. Most laboratories have requirements that students are expected to follow such as:

- All students should behave in a responsible manner

- Students should follow all written and verbal instructions, always asking for help if uncertain about how to proceed or use any equipment

- Students must never work without the presence of an instructor

- There must be absolutely no eating, drinking, smoking, application of cosmetics, chewing gum, food containers, or drug use of any kind

- Students must always wash their hands after handling any chemicals or specimens

- Protective clothing must be worn when instructed

- Students must not touch any equipment, chemicals, or specimens until instructed to do so

- All work areas must be kept clean at all times

- Students must never leave an experiment unattended

Appropriate Laboratory Apparel and Conduct

Protective Clothing

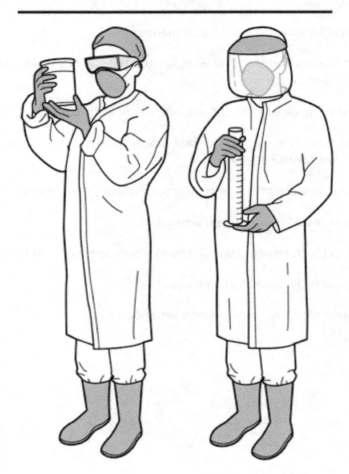

Special clothing requirements may be necessary depending on the task and its potential hazards. In general, students in the lab should:

- Wear long sleeves, long pants, and closed-toed shoes.

- Tuck in all loose or baggy clothing.

- If handling harmful chemicals, wear lab coats or jumpsuits to protect clothing. To protect the hands, wear latex gloves, which should be disposed of after each use.

- If clothing becomes saturated in chemicals, immediately remove clothing and dispose of or decontaminate the article prior to laundering; however. It is never recommended to wash contaminated clothing at home.

- Wear safety goggles when handling hazardous chemicals or when doing tasks that may require exposure to high-intensity light or flames.

Emergency Procedures

Instructors should follow the appropriate procedures in the event of an emergency.

Fires
- If anyone catches on fire, don't allow them to run around in panic. Grab the nearest fire blanket, or have them stop, drop, and roll.

- If a student is burned, apply ice packs to the burned areas, and wrap the person in a warm blanket to prevent shock.

- If the fire is small, use a fire extinguisher as outlined previously, or place a nonflammable container over the fire to smother it.

- If the fire is too large to fight, calmly tell students to leave all of their belongings and exit the room, following the building's evacuation plan.

- If possible, move any flammable objects out of the way and power off any devices. Close the door to contain the fire.

- Pull the closest fire alarm and notify Public Safety.

Chemical Spills
The following guidelines illustrate the appropriate procedures in the event of a chemical spill:

- Chemical spills should only be cleaned up under the following conditions:

- The spill is of a known material.
- There is appropriate protection available, i.e., gloves, eye googles, lab coat, etc.
- The spill is minor.
- The spill is not of highly-toxic materials.

- Anyone who has been saturated by a toxic chemical must remove their clothes and/or proceed to a safety shower.

- Drains must be protected using a barrier or absorbent material.

- Waste must be disposed as described previously.

Handling of Injuries
In the event of a major medical injury, an instructor should:

- Remain calm
- Call 9-1-1
- If the person is not breathing, attempt CPR
- Keep the person warm to avoid shock
- Don't attempt to move the person unless staying put would harm them further

For a minor medical emergency, all laboratories should come equipped with a first-aid kit. A first-aid kit can be used for the following injuries:

- Minor cuts and puncture wounds
- The cut should be washed thoroughly with soap and water before applying the bandage.
- Minor burns
- The burn should be run under cold water before applying the bandage.
- Scrapes
- Insect bites or stings
- Sprains
- Allergies

All injuries, however minor, must be reported to a superior.

Major Historical Developments in Science

Accepted Principles and Models Develop Over Time

The very nature of scientific knowledge is that it continues to build upon itself with constant experimentation and newfound discoveries, throwing out old theories that have been proven false and replacing them with new ones. By using principles that have been developed and tested over hundreds of years, scientists and engineers have created today's technology.

Records of scientific experimentation date back as far as 400 B.C.E., although most significant discoveries didn't occur until the 17th century. A timeline of major accepted principles and models—which is by no means exhaustive—is listed below, and displays theories that were developed, discarded, and built upon:

- 1543 –Nicolaus Copernicus developed the Heliocentric Model of the Solar System
- 1609—Galileo Galilei made telescopic observations of the Solar System
- 1619—Johannes Kepler completed the laws of planetary motion
- 1622—Robert Boyle developed the law of ideal gas, which states that the pressure of an ideal gas is inversely proportional to the volume it occupies
- 1665—Robert Hook discovered the biological cell
- 1672 - 1687—Sir Isaac Newton discovered that white light is a spectrum of different-colored rays, developed calculus, and created mathematical descriptions of force, gravity, and the laws of motion
- 1751—Benjamin Franklin discovered that lightning is electrical
- 1778 - 1798—Antoine Lavoisier discovered "phlogiston," later identified as oxygen; developed the law of conservation of mass and the basis for chemistry
- 1781-1800—William Herschel discovered Uranus, expanding the boundaries of the known universe and discovered infrared radiation
- 1820—Hans Christian Ørsted discovered the relationship between electricity and the magnetic field using a compass
- 1843—James Prescott Joule created the first law of thermodynamics
- 1858—Rudolf Virchow discovered that cells can only come from pre-existing cells
- 1859—Charles Darwin and Alfred Wallace developed the theory of evolution by natural selection

- 1864—James Clerk Maxwell developed the theory of electromagnetism
- 1865—Gregor Mendel identified the laws of genetic inheritance and provided the basis for genetics
- 1869—Dmitri Mendeleev create the periodic table of elements
- 1887—Alfred A. Michelson and Edward W. Morley disproved the existence of "the aether"
- 1897—J. J. Thomson discovered the electron
- 1900—Max Planck created the law of black body radiation and the basis for quantum theory.
- 1905-1915—Albert Einstein developed theories of special relativity, the photoelectric effect, and general relativity
- 1911—Ernest Rutherford discovered the nucleus
- 1912—Alfred Wegner proposed continental drift, the basis for plate tectonics
- 1913—Neils Bohr created a model of the atom
- 1924—Edwin Hubble realized the Milky Way is just one of many galaxies
- 1925-1928—Major developments in quantum mechanics
- 1927—Georges Lamaitre proposed the Big Bang Theory
- 1928—Alexander Fleming discovered penicillin
- 1952—Jonas Salk developed and tested the polio vaccine
- 1953—Rosalind Franklin, Francis Crick, and James Watson discovered the helical structure of DNA
- 1983—Kary Mullis invented polymerase chain reactions
- 1997—Roslin Institute cloned the sheep Dolly
- 2001—First draft of the Human Genome Project was published
- 2006—Shinya Yamanaka generated the first induced pluripotent stem cells
- 2015—Traces of liquid water found on Mars

Major Developments in Science

Certain discoveries that revolutionized scientific understanding deserve a deeper look.

Atomic Theory
Atomic theory—a philosophical concept in ancient Greece that solidified in the 19th century—states that the universe is made up of discrete units called *atoms*. Initially believed to have been one inseparable unit, the atom was discovered to be composed of subatomic particles—protons, electrons, and neutrons—in which the protons and neutrons comprise a dense nucleus and the electrons orbit around it at mind-boggling distances. The atom is now believed to be composed of mostly space.

The Heliocentric Model of the Solar System
Before Nicolaus Copernicus, people believed the Earth was the center of the universe. Copernicus placed the Sun at the center of the Solar System, with the other planets revolving around it. At the time, only Mercury, Venus, Earth, Mars, Saturn, and Jupiter were known. Evidence suggests that the ancient Greeks also used a heliocentric model of the solar system in the 3rd century B.C.E.

Gravity
Sir Isaac Newton recognized that gravity was responsible for objects falling toward the ground, which he extrapolated into a law that concluded that every object in the universe is attracted to another object through a force that is directly proportional to the product of their masses and inversely proportional to

the square of the distance between them. This is called the law of universal gravitation and is expressed via the following formula:

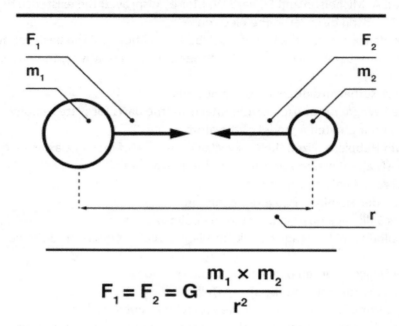

The Law of Universal Gravitation

$$F_1 = F_2 = G\ \frac{m_1 \times m_2}{r^2}$$

Evolution

In 1859, Charles Darwin proposed the theory of evolution by natural selection, which explained how organisms developed *very* gradually over time as a result of mutations that enhanced an organism's ability to survive.

Key points of the theory of evolution include:

- There is genetic variation among species—meaning every species has a distinct arrangement of genes.

- Natural selection is the result of a random mutation that occurs in the genome and is favorable to the survival of the organism. For example, a random mutation that causes a moth's wings to appear white, making it harder for birds to eat them because they can't spot them against white tree branches, has a better chance of survival than dark moths. The birds eat the dark moths instead, and the white moth survives to pass on its mutation.

- The random mutation must be heritable—that is, it must be able to be passed on to its offspring.

- Natural selection is not the idea that organisms evolved to fit to their environment. For example, assuming that giraffes developed long necks to eat from tall trees is erroneous.

Continental Drift (Plate Tectonics)

In 1912, Alfred Wegener proposed that at one point in Earth's history, all of the continents were joined in one supercontinent (now known as Pangaea) and gradually separated to form the seven separate continents as they currently exist. The evidence, he argued, was present in the fact that fossils of similar species were found on continents several thousand miles apart. Unfortunately, Wegener had no model to explain the mechanism in which this occurred, so his theory was discarded.

However, Wegener's proposal was the foundation for plate tectonics, the theory that the Earth's crust is composed of rigid, moving rock plates called the *lithosphere*. They move by gliding slowly over the Earth's outer *mantle*, a layer of slowly moving silicate rock propelled by the hot magma below it. As hot rock from the Earth's core rises to the surface, it causes the fragmented pieces of the crust to spread apart, moving away from each other. As the hot rock begins to cool, it sinks towards the Earth's core, causing the plates above it to sink as well, meanwhile pushing the adjacent plates over the sinking plates. The deep trench created by the sinking and pushing is called the *subduction zone*. This process of spreading and sinking is the underlying cause of the movement of the continents.

Subduction

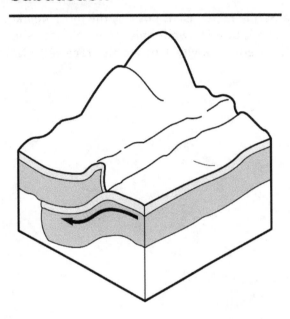

Contributions of Major Historical Figures

Many of the greatest contributors to the advancement of scientific knowledge were mentioned above. However, a brief overview of the most influential scientists is below.

Galileo Galilei
Galileo Galilei (1564-1642), considered by many to be the "Father of Modern Science," was an Italian astronomer, physicist, and philosopher. His telescopic investigations provided the basis for observational astronomy, in which he confirmed the phases of Venus, four of Jupiter's major moons, and sunspots.

Isaac Newton
Isaac Newton (1643-1727) was an English mathematician, physicist, astronomer, and philosopher. His most influential contributions were the theory of gravitation, the theory of color, the development of calculus, and the three natural laws of motion.

Charles Darwin

Charles Darwin (1809-1882) was an English biologist, whose major contributions include his theory of evolution as a result of natural selection, which provided a unifying theory for the genetic relationship and diversity of all species on Earth.

Max Planck

Max Planck (1858-1947) was a German physicist and the founder of quantum theory, a branch of theoretical physics that focuses on the relationships between subatomic particles.

Niels Bohr

Niels Bohr (1885-1962) was a Danish physicist primarily responsible for the creation of the nuclear model of the atom, which illustrates that electrons orbit around the atom's nucleus. His work received the Nobel Prize in Physics in 1922.

Albert Einstein

Albert Einstein (1879-1955), a German scientist, is possibly the most well-known scientist and contributor to modern physics. He is best known for his theory of mass-energy equivalence ($E = mc^2$) and his theories of special and general relativity. Einstein also received a Nobel Prize in Physics in 1921.

Practice Questions

1. A scientist is trying to determine how much poison will kill a rat the fastest. Which of the following statements is an example of an appropriate hypothesis?
   a. Rats that are given lots of poison seem to die quickly.
   b. Does the amount of poison affect how quickly the rat dies?
   c. The more poison a rat is given, the quicker it will die.
   d. Poison is fatal to rats.

2. In testing how quickly a rat dies by the amount of poison it eats, which of the following is the independent variable and which is the dependent variable?
   a. How quickly the rat dies is the independent variable; the amount of poison is the dependent variable.
   b. The amount of poison is the independent variable; how quickly the rat dies is the dependent variable.
   c. Whether the rat eats the poison is the independent variable; how quickly the rat dies is the dependent variable.
   d. The cage the rat is kept in is the independent variable; the amount of poison is the dependent variable.

3. Which of the following is a representation of a natural pattern or occurrence that's difficult or impossible to experience directly?
   a. A theory
   b. A model
   c. A law
   d. An observation

4. Which of the following is a standard or series of standards to which the results from an experiment are compared?
   a. A control
   b. A variable
   c. A constant
   d. Collected data

5. "This flower is dead; someone must have forgotten to water it." This statement is an example of which of the following?
   a. A classification
   b. An observation
   c. An inference
   d. A collection

6. How many centimeters is 0.78 kilometers?
   a. 7.8 cm
   b. 0.078 cm
   c. 78,000 cm
   d. 780 cm

7. 4.67 miles is equivalent to how many kilometers to three significant digits?
    a. 7.514 km
    b. 7.51 km
    c. 2.90 km
    d. 2.902 km

8. Which of the following correctly displays 8,600,000,000,000 in scientific notation (to two significant figures)?
    a. 8.6×10^{12}
    b. 8.6×10^{-12}
    c. 8.6×10^{11}
    d. 8.60×10^{12}

9. The number 0.00067 has how many significant figures?
    a. Six
    b. Five
    c. Three
    d. Two

10. The acceleration of a falling object due to gravity has been proven to be 9.8 m/s^2. A scientist drops a cactus four times and measures the acceleration with an accelerometer and gets the following results: 9.79 m/s^2, 9.81 m/s^2, 9.80 m/s^2, and 9.78 m/s^2. Which of the following accurately describes the measurements?
    a. They're both accurate and precise.
    b. They're accurate but not precise.
    c. They're precise but not accurate.
    d. They're neither accurate nor precise.

11. Which is the correct value for the mean of the following numbers to the appropriate number of significant figures: 3.2, 7.5, 9.6, and 5.4?
    a. 6.4
    b. 6.42
    c. 6.425
    d. 6

12. The following graph demonstrates which type of correlation?

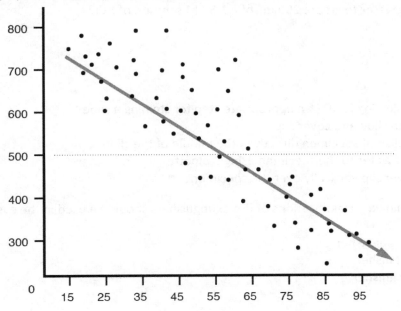

   a. Positive correlation
   b. No correlation
   c. Negative correlation
   d. Zero correlation

13. Which of the following is NOT a correct way to handle chemicals or specimens?
   a. Always read the safety and data sheets that accompany a product.
   b. Don't use substitutions for any chemicals.
   c. Keep all work stations clean and sanitized.
   d. Always handle chemicals near safety equipment.

14. Which of the following shouldn't be stored in metal?
   a. Acids and bases
   b. Hydrofluoric gas
   c. Gasoline
   d. Dihydrogen monoxide

15. How many grams of solid $CaCO_3$ are needed to make 600 mL of a 0.35 M solution? The atomic masses for the elements are as follows: Ca = 40.07 g/mol; C = 12.01 g/mol; O = 15.99 g/mol.
   a. 18.3 g
   b. 19.7 g
   c. 21.0 g
   d. 24.2 g

16. How many mL (to the appropriate number of significant figures) of a 12.0 M stock solution of HCl should be added to water to create 250 mL of a 1.50 M solution of HCl?
   a. 31.25 mL
   b. 32 mL
   c. 30 mL
   d. 31.3 mL

17. Which of the following is NOT an appropriate step for staining a slide?
   a. Obtain a clean slide and cover slip
   b. Place a thin slice of specimen directly in the middle of the slide
   c. Add a drop of water to the specimen using a pipette
   d. Place the cover slip vertically over the specimen

18. Which of the following classifications of fire extinguishers should be used in the event of an electrical fire?
   I. An ABC extinguisher
   II. A B Extinguisher
   III. A C Extinguisher
   a. I
   b. II
   c. III
   d. I & III

19. The model of an atom, in which electrons move around a dense nucleus in a fixed orbit, is derived from which of the following theories?
   a. The heliocentric model of the solar system
   b. The theory of gravitation
   c. Atomic theory
   d. The theory of atomic evolution

20. Which of the following scientists contributed the theory of gravitation, the theory of color, and the major laws of motion?
   a. Charles Darwin
   b. Albert Einstein
   c. Max Planck
   d. Isaac Newton

Answer Explanations

1. C: A hypothesis is a statement that makes a prediction between two variables. The two variables here are the amount of poison and how quickly the rat dies. Choice *C* states that the more poison a rat is given, the more quickly it will die, which is a prediction. Choice *A* is incorrect because it's simply an observation. Choice *B* is incorrect because it's a question posed by the observation but makes no predictions. Choice *D* is incorrect because it's simply a fact.

2. B: The independent variable is the variable manipulated and the dependent variable is the result of the changes in the independent variable. Choice *B* is correct because the amount of poison is the variable that is changed, and the speed of rat death is the result of the changes in the amount of poison administered. Choice *A* is incorrect because that answer states the opposite. Choice *C* is false because the scientist isn't attempting to determine whether the rat will die *if* it eats poison; the scientist is testing how quickly the rat will die depending on *how much* poison it eats. Choice *D* is incorrect because the cage isn't manipulated in any way and has nothing to do with the hypothesis.

3. B: Models are representations of concepts that are impossible to experience directly, such as the 3D representation of DNA, so Choice *B* is correct. Choice *A* is incorrect because theories simply explain why things happen. Choice *C* is incorrect because laws describe how things happen. Choice *D* is false because an observation analyzes situations using human senses.

4. A: A control is the component or group of the experimental design that isn't manipulated—it's the standard against which the resultant findings are compared, so Choice *A* is correct. A variable is an element of the experiment that is able to be manipulated, making Choice *B* false. A constant is a condition of the experiment outside of the hypothesis that remains unchanged in order to isolate the changes in the variables; therefore, Choice *C* is incorrect. Choice *D* is false because collected data are simply recordings of the observed phenomena that result from the experiment.

5. C: An inference is a logical prediction of a why an event occurred based on previous experiences or education. The person in this example knows that plants need water to survive; therefore, the prediction that someone forgot to water the plant is a reasonable inference, hence Choice *C* is correct. A classification is the grouping of events or objects into categories, so Choice *A* is false. An observation analyzes situations using human senses, so Choice *B* is false. Choice *D* is incorrect because collecting is the act of gathering data for analysis.

6. C: Conversion within the metric system is as simple as the movement of decimal points. The prefix *kilo-* means "one thousand," or three zeros, so the procedure to convert kilometers to the primary unit (meters) is to move the decimal point three units to the right. To get to centimeters, the decimal point must be moved an additional two places to the right: 0.78 → 78,000. Choice *A* is false because the decimal point has only been moved one place to right. Choice *B* is incorrect because the decimal point is moved two units in the wrong direction. Choice *D* is false because the decimal has only been moved three units to the right. The problem can also be solved by using the following conversion equation:

$$0.78 \ km \ \times \frac{1,000 \ m}{1 \ km} \times \frac{100 \ cm}{1 \ m} = 78,000 \ cm$$

The kilometer (km) units cancel each other out, as do the meter (m) units. The only units left are centimeters (cm).

7. B: The answer choices for this question are tricky. Converting to kilometers from miles will yield the choice 7.514 when using the conversion 1 mile = 1.609 km. However, because the value in miles is written to three significant figures, the answer choice should also yield a value in three significant figures, making 7.51 km the correct answer. Choices *C* and *D* could seem correct if someone flipped the conversion upside-down—that is, if they divided by 1.609 instead of multiplied by it.

$$4.67mi \times \frac{1.609km}{1mi} = 7.514 \ or \ 7.51$$

8. A: The decimal point for this value is located after the final zero. Because the decimal is moved 12 places to the left in order to get it between the *8* and the *6*, then the resulting exponent is positive, so Choice *A* is the correct answer. Choice *B* is false because the decimal has been moved in the wrong direction. Choice *C* is incorrect because the decimal has been moved an incorrect number of times. Choice *D* is false because this value is written to three significant figures, not two.

$$8,\underset{12}{\underbrace{6}}\underset{11}{\underbrace{0}}\underset{10}{\underbrace{0}}\underset{9}{\underbrace{}},\underset{8}{\underbrace{0}}\underset{7}{\underbrace{0}}\underset{6}{\underbrace{0}},\underset{5}{\underbrace{0}}\underset{4}{\underbrace{0}}\underset{3}{\underbrace{0}},\underset{2}{\underbrace{0}}\underset{1}{\underbrace{0}}0$$

9. D: Leading zeros (those present after a decimal) are never significant, while all non-zero digits are significant. Therefore, in the value 0.00067, the only significant figures are 6 and 7, so this value has only two significant figures, making Choice *D* correct. Choices *A*, *B*, and *C* assume that all or some of the zeros are significant, so these options are incorrect.

10. B: The set of results is close to the actual value of the acceleration due to gravity, making the results accurate. However, there is a different value recorded every time, so the results aren't precise, which makes Choice *B* the correct answer.

11. A: To find the mean, the sum of the values can be calculated and then divided by the number of values. To report the result to the appropriate number of significant figures, the number of significant figures in which the values were given must be identified. In this case, every value is given at two significant figures. When the values are added and divided by four, they yield a value of 6.425. However, because the values are given in two significant figures, then the answer is 6.4. Choices *B*, *C*, and *D* give an incorrect number of significant figures.

$$\frac{3.2 + 7.5 + 9.6 + 5.4}{4} = 6.4$$

12. C: The graph shows that as the value of x increases, the value of y decreases, which is the definition of a negative correlation, so Choice *C* is correct. A positive correlation is when the value of y increases as the value of x increases, so Choice *A* is incorrect. Choices *B* and *D* both show no determinable relationship between two variables.

13. B: It's actually highly recommended to use substitutions for any harmful chemicals for educational purposes, so Choice *B* is the correct answer. Choices *A*, *C*, and *D* are all proper ways to handle chemicals and specimens.

14. A: Acids and bases should not be stored in metal, as they will corrode it. All the other listed substances can be stored in metal (note that dihydrogen monoxide is the scientific name for water).

15. C: To make a solution from a pure solid, the total molecular weight of the substance must be calculated and then the proper mass of the substance in grams must be added to water to make a solution. To calculate the total molecular weight, the individual molecular weights must be added. Finally, the mass of substance needed to make the solution can be calculated.

$$600mL\ CaCO_3 \times \frac{0.350\ m*l}{1000mL} \times \frac{100g\ CaCO_3}{1mol\ CaCO_3} = 21g\ CaCO_3$$

The calculations reveal that Choice C is the correct answer. All other reported values are incorrect.

16. D: Preparing a solution from a stock is simply a process of dilution by adding water to a certain amount of the stock. The amount of stock to use can be calculated using a formula and algebra:

$$V_S = \frac{M_D V_D}{M_S}$$

$$M_D = 1.5$$

$$V_D = 250ml$$

$$M_S = 12.0M$$

$$V_S = \frac{(1.5M)(250ml)}{12.0M} = 31.3ml$$

Because the given values are written to three significant figures, the answer should also be written in three significant figures, making Choice D the correct answer. The other answer choices are either incorrect values or reported to an incorrect number of significant figures.

17. D: A cover slip should be lowered at a 45° angle to the specimen, not vertically, so Choice D is the correct answer. The other answer choices describe correct procedures involved in staining a slide.

18. D: Class C fires are caused by electricity. Any fire extinguisher with C would be acceptable to use to smother a minor fire, so Choice D is the correct answer, as both ABC and C fire extinguishers would be okay. B fire extinguishers are only used for fires caused by liquid or gaseous flammables, such as gasoline or carbon dioxide, so Choice B is not the correct answer.

19. C: Atomic theory states that an atom is composed of a nucleus and subatomic particles, in which electrons orbit around the nucleus that contains protons and neutrons, so Choice C is the correct answer. Choice A is false because it's a model, not a theory, and has to do with the Solar System and not with atoms. Choice B is false because the theory of gravitation is the notion that all particles in the universe are attracted to one another depending on their mass and distance. Choice D is incorrect because there's no such thing as the theory of atomic evolution.

20. D: Isaac Newton is most famous for his contributions to science through the theory of gravitation, the theory of color, and laws of motion, which makes Choice D the correct answer. Charles Darwin is responsible for the theory of evolution by natural selection, so Choice A is incorrect. Albert Einstein is most famous for his theory of mass-energy equivalence and theories of relativity, so Choice B isn't the correct answer. Finally, Max Planck was the originator of quantum theory and the processes that occur at the subatomic level; thus, Choice C is also incorrect.

Physical Science

Basic Principles

Structure of Matter

Elements, Compounds, and Mixtures

Everything that takes up space and has mass is composed of *matter*. Understanding the basic characteristics and properties of matter helps with classification and identification.

An *element* is a substance that cannot be chemically decomposed to a simpler substance, while still retaining the properties of the element.

Compounds are composed of two or more elements that are chemically combined. The constituent elements in the compound are in constant proportions by mass.

When a material can be separated by physicals means (such as sifting it through a colander), it is called a *mixture*. Mixtures are categorized into two types: *heterogeneous* and *homogeneous*. Heterogeneous mixtures have physically distinct parts, which retain their different properties. A mix of salt and sugar is an example of a heterogeneous mixture. With heterogenous mixtures, it is possible that different samples from the same parent mixture may have different proportions of each component in the mixture. For example, in the sugar and salt mixture, there may be uneven mixing of the two, causing one random tablespoon sample to be mostly salt, while a different tablespoon sample may be mostly sugar.

A homogeneous mixture, also called a *solution*, has uniform properties throughout a given sample. An example of a homogeneous solution is salt fully dissolved in warm water. In this case, any number of samples taken from the parent solution would be identical.

Atoms, Molecules, and Ions

The basic building blocks of matter are *atoms*, which are extremely small particles that retain their identity during chemical reactions. Atoms can be singular or grouped to form elements. Elements are composed of one type of atom with the same properties.

Molecules are a group of atoms—either the same or different types—that are chemically bonded together by attractive forces. For example, hydrogen and oxygen are both atoms but, when bonded together, form water.

Ions are electrically-charged particles that are formed from an atom or a group of atoms via the loss or gain of electrons.

Basic Properties of Solids, Liquids, and Gases

Matter exists in certain *states*, or physical forms, under different conditions. These states are called *solid*, *liquid*, or *gas*.

A solid has a rigid, or set, form and occupies a fixed shape and volume. Solids generally maintain their shape when exposed to outside forces.

Liquids and gases are considered fluids, which have no set shape. Liquids are fluid, yet are distinguished from gases by their incompressibility (incapable of being compressed) and set volume. Liquids can be transferred from one container to another, but cannot be forced to fill containers of different volumes via compression without causing damage to the container. For example, if one attempts to force a given volume or number of particles of a liquid, such as water, into a fixed container, such as a small water bottle, the container would likely explode from the extra water.

A gas can easily be compressed into a confined space, such as a tire or an air mattress. Gases have no fixed shape or volume. They can also be subjected to outside forces, and the number of gas molecules that can fill a certain volume vary with changes in temperature and pressure.

Basic Structure of an Atom

Atomic Models
Theories of the atomic model have developed over the centuries. The most commonly referenced model of an atom was proposed by Niels Bohr. Bohr studied the models of J.J. Thomson and Ernest Rutherford and adapted his own theories from these existing models. Bohr compared the structure of the atom to that of the Solar System, where there is a center, or nucleus, with various sized orbitals circulating around this nucleus. This is a simplified version of what scientists have discovered about atoms, including the structures and placements of any orbitals. Modern science has made further adaptations to the model, including the fact that orbitals are actually made of electron "clouds."

Atomic Structure: Nucleus, Electrons, Protons, and Neutrons
Following the Bohr model of the atom, the nucleus, or core, is made up of positively charged *protons* and neutrally charged *neutrons*. The neutrons are theorized to be in the nucleus with the protons to provide greater "balance" at the center of the atom. The nucleus of the atom makes up the majority (more than 99%) of the mass of an atom, while the orbitals surrounding the nucleus contain negatively charged *electrons*. The entire structure of an atom is incredibly small.

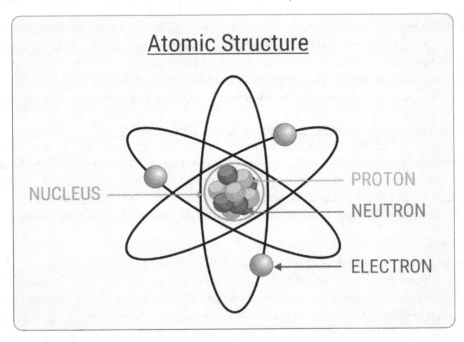

Atomic Structure

NUCLEUS

PROTON

NEUTRON

ELECTRON

Atomic Number, Atomic Mass, and Isotopes

The *atomic number* of an atom is determined by the number of protons within the nucleus. When a substance is composed of atoms that all have the same atomic number, it is called an *element*. Elements are arranged by atomic number and grouped by properties in the *periodic table*.

An atom's *mass number* is determined by the sum of the total number of protons and neutrons in the atom. Most nuclei have a net neutral charge, and all atoms of one type have the same atomic number. However, there are some atoms of the same type that have a different mass number, due to an imbalance of neutrons. These are called *isotopes*. In isotopes, the atomic number, which is determined by the number of protons, is the same, but the mass number, which is determined by adding the protons and neutrons, is different due to the irregular number of neutrons.

Electron Arrangements

Electrons are most easily organized into distributions of subshells called *electron configurations*. Subshells fill from the inside (closest to the nucleus) to the outside. Therefore, once a subshell is filled, the next shell farther from the nucleus begins to fill, and so on. Atoms with electrons on the outside of a noble gas core (an atom with an electron inner shell that corresponds to the configuration of one of the noble gases, such as Neon) and pseudo-noble gas core (an atom with an electron inner shell that is similar to that of a noble gas core along with $(n-1) d^{10}$ electrons), are called *valence* electrons. Valence electrons are primarily the electrons involved in chemical reactions. The similarities in their configurations account for similarities in properties of groups of elements. Essentially, the groups (vertical columns) on the periodic table all have similar characteristics, such as solubility and reactivity, due to their similar electron configurations.

Basic Characteristics of Radioactive Materials

Radioisotopes

As mentioned, an isotope is a variation of an element with a different number of neutrons in the nucleus, causing the nucleus to be unstable. When an element is unstable, it will go through decay or disintegration. All manmade elements are unstable and will break down. The length of time for an unstable element to break down is called the *half-life*. As an element breaks down, it forms other elements, known as daughters. Once a stable daughter is formed, the radioactive decay stops.

Characteristics of Alpha Particles, Beta Particles, and Gamma Radiation

As radioactive decay is occurring, the unstable element emits *alpha*, *beta*, and *gamma* radiation. Alpha and beta radiation are not as far-reaching or as powerful as gamma radiation. Alpha radiation is caused by the emission of two protons and two neutrons, while beta radiation is caused by the emission of either an electron or a positron. In contrast, gamma radiation is the release of photons of energy, not particles. This makes it the farthest-reaching and the most dangerous of these emissions.

Fission and Fusion

The splitting of an atom is referred to as fission, whereas the combination of two atoms into one is called fusion. To achieve fission and break apart an isotope, the unstable isotope is bombarded with high-speed particles. This process releases a large amount of energy and is what provides the energy in a nuclear power plant. Fusion occurs when two nuclei are merged to form a larger nucleus. The action of fusion also creates a tremendous amount of energy. To put the difference in the levels of energy between fission and fusion into perspective, the level of energy from fusion is what provides energy to the Earth's sun.

Basic Concepts and Relationships Involving Energy and Matter

The study of energy and matter, including heat and temperature, is called *thermodynamics*. There are four fundamental laws of thermodynamics, but the first two are the most commonly discussed.

First Law of Thermodynamics
The first law of thermodynamics is also known as the *conservation of energy*. This law states that energy cannot be created or destroyed, but is just transferred or converted into another form through a thermodynamic process. For example, if a liquid is boiled and then removed from the heat source, the liquid will eventually cool. This change in temperature is not because of a loss of energy or heat, but from a transfer of energy or heat to the surroundings. This can include the heating of nearby air molecules, or the transfer of heat from the liquid to the container or to the surface where the container is resting.

This law also applies to the idea of perpetual motion. A self-powered perpetual motion machine cannot exist. This is because the motion of the machine would inevitably lose some heat or energy to friction, whether from materials or from the air.

Second Law of Thermodynamics
The second law of thermodynamics is also known as the *law of entropy*. Entropy means chaos or disorder. In simple terms, this law means that all systems tend toward chaos. When one or more systems interacts with another, the total entropy is the sum of the interacting systems, and this overall sum also tends toward entropy.

Conservation of Matter in Chemical Systems
The conservation of energy is seen in the conservation of matter in chemical systems. This is helpful when attempting to understand chemical processes, since these processes must balance out. This means that extra matter cannot be created or destroyed, it must all be accounted for through a chemical process.

Kinetic and Potential Energy
The conservation of energy also applies to the study of energy in physics. This is clearly demonstrated through the kinetic and potential energy involved in a system.

The energy of motion is called *kinetic energy*. If an object has height, or is raised above the ground, it has *potential energy*. The total energy of any given system is the sum of the potential energy and the kinetic energy of the subject (object) in the system.

Potential energy is expressed by the equation:

$$PE = mgh$$

Where m equals the object's mass, g equals acceleration caused by the gravitational force acting on the object, and h equals the height of the object above the ground.

Kinetic energy is expressed by the following equation:

$$KE = \tfrac{1}{2}\, mv^2$$

Where m is the mass of the object and v is the velocity of the object.

Conservation of energy allows the total energy for any situation to be calculated by the following equation:

KE + PE

For example, a roller coaster poised at the top of a hill has all potential energy, and when it reaches the bottom of that hill, as it is speeding through its lowest point, it has all kinetic energy. Halfway down the hill, the total energy of the roller coaster is about half potential energy and half kinetic energy. Therefore, the total energy is found by calculating both the potential energy and the kinetic energy and then adding them together.

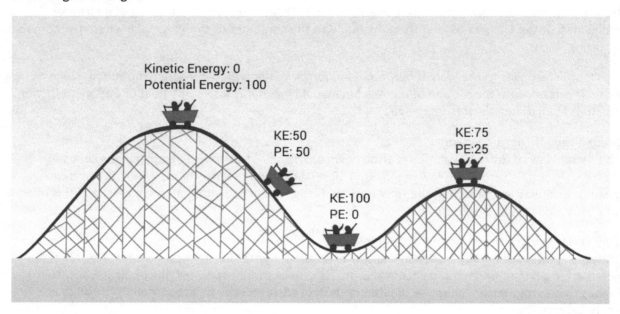

Transformations Between Different Forms of Energy

As stated by the conservation of energy, energy cannot be created or destroyed. If a system gains or loses energy, it is transformed within a single system from one type of energy to another or transferred from one system to another. For example, if the roller coaster system has potential energy that transfers to kinetic energy, the kinetic energy can then be transferred into thermal energy or heat released through braking as the coaster descends the hill. Energy can also transform from the chemical energy inside of a battery into the electrical energy that lights a train set. The energy released through nuclear fusion (when atoms are joined together, they release heat) is what supplies power plants with the energy for electricity. All energy is transferred from one form to another through different reactions. It can also be transferred through the simple action of atoms bumping into each other, causing a transfer of heat.

Differences Between Chemical and Physical Properties/Changes

A change in the physical form of matter, but not in its chemical identity, is known as a *physical change*. An example of a physical change is tearing a piece of paper in half. This changes the shape of the matter, but it is still paper.

Conversely, a *chemical change* alters the chemical composition or identity of matter. An example of a chemical change is burning a piece of paper. The heat necessary to burn the paper alters the chemical composition of the paper. This chemical change cannot be easily undone, since it has created at least one form of matter different than the original matter.

Temperature Scales

There are three main temperature scales used in science. The scale most often used in the United States is the *Fahrenheit* scale. This scale is based on the measurement of water freezing at 32° F and water boiling at 212° F. The Celsius scale uses 0° C as the temperature for water freezing and 100° C for water boiling. The accepted measurement by the International System of Units (from the French *Système international d'unités*), or SI, for temperature is the Kelvin scale. This is the scale employed in thermodynamics, since its zero is the basis for *absolute zero*, or the unattainable temperature, when matter no longer exhibits degradation.

The conversions between the temperature scales are as follows:

$$°Fahrenheit\ to\ °Celsius: {}^{0}C = \frac{5}{9}({}^{0}F - 32)$$

$$°Celsius\ to\ °Fahrenheit: {}^{0}F = \frac{9}{5}({}^{0}C) + 32$$

$$°Celsius\ to\ Kelvin: K = {}^{0}C + 273.15$$

Transfer of Thermal Energy and Its Basic Measurement

There are three basic ways in which energy is transferred. The first is through *radiation*. Radiation is transmitted through electromagnetic waves and it does not need a medium to travel (it can travel in a vacuum). This is how the sun warms the Earth, and typically applies to large objects with great amounts of heat or objects with a large difference in their heat measurements.

The second form of heat transfer is *convection*. Convection involves the movement of "fluids" from one place to another. (The term *fluid* does not necessarily apply to a liquid, but any substance in which the molecules can slide past each other, such as gases.) It is this movement that transfers the heat to or from an area. Generally, convective heat transfer occurs through diffusion, which is when heat moves from areas of higher concentrations of particles to those of lower concentrations of particles and less heat. This process of flowing heat can be assisted or amplified through the use of fans and other methods of forcing the molecules to move.

The final process is called *conduction*. Conduction involves transferring heat through the touching of molecules. Molecules can either bump into each other to transfer heat, or they may already be touching each other and transfer the heat through this connection. For example, imagine a circular burner on an electric stove top. The coil begins to glow orange near the base of the burner that is connected to the stove because it heats up first. Since the burner is one continuous piece of metal, the molecules are touching each other. As they pass heat along the coil, it begins to glow all the way to the end.

To determine the amount of heat required to warm the coil in the above example, the type of material from which the coil is made must be known. The quantity of heat required to raise one gram of a substance one degree Celsius (or Kelvin) at a constant pressure is called *specific heat*. This measurement can be calculated for masses of varying substances by using the following equation:

$$q = s \times m \times \Delta t$$

Where q is the specific heat, s is the specific heat of the material being used, m is the mass of the substance being used, and Δt is the change in temperature.

A calorimeter is used to measure the heat of a reaction (either expelled or absorbed) and the temperature changes in a controlled system. A simple calorimeter can be made by using an insulated coffee cup with a thermometer inside. For this example, a lid of some sort would be preferred to prevent any escaping heat that could be lost by evaporation or convection.

Applications of Energy and Matter Relationships

When considering the cycling of matter in ecosystems, the flow of energy and atoms is from one organism to another. The *trophic level* of an organism refers to its position in a food chain. The level shows the relationship between it and other organisms on the same level and how they use and transfer energy to other levels in the food chain. This includes consumption and decomposition for the transfer of energy among organisms and matter. The sun provides energy through radiation to the Earth, and plants convert this light energy into chemical energy, which is then released to fuel the organism's activities.

Naturally occurring elements deep within the Earth's mantle release heat during their radioactive decay. This release of heat drives convection currents in the Earth's magma, which then drives plate tectonics. The transfer of heat from these actions causes the plates to move and create convection currents in the oceans. This type of cycling can also be seen in transformations of rocks. Sedimentary rocks can undergo significant amounts of heat and pressure to become metamorphic rocks. These rocks can melt back into magma, which then becomes igneous rock or, with extensive weathering and erosion, can revert to sediment and form sedimentary rocks over time. Under the right conditions (weathering and erosion), igneous rocks can also become sediment, which eventually compresses into sedimentary rock. Erosion helps the process by redepositing rocks into sediment on the sea floor.

All of these cycles are examples of the transfer of energy from one type into another, along with the conservation of mass from one level to the next.

Chemistry

Periodicity and States of Matter

Periodic Table of the Elements
Using the periodic table, elements are arranged by atomic number, similar characteristics, and electron configurations in a tabular format. The columns, called *groups*, are sorted by similar chemical properties and characteristics such as appearance and reactivity. This can be seen in the shiny texture of metals, the high melting points of alkali Earth metals, and the softness of post-transition metals. The rows are arranged by electron valance configurations and are called *periods*.

The elements are set in ascending order from left to right by atomic number. As mentioned, the atomic number is the number of protons contained within the nucleus of the atom. For example, the element helium has an atomic number of 2 because it has two protons in its nucleus.

An element's mass number is calculated by adding the number of protons and neutrons of an atom together, while the atomic mass of an element is the weighted average of the naturally occurring atoms of a given element, or the relative abundance of isotopes that might be used in chemistry. For example, the atomic (mass) number of chlorine is 35; however, the atomic mass of chlorine is 35.5 amu (atomic mass unit). This discrepancy exists because there are many isotopes (meaning the nucleus could have 36 instead of 35 protons) occurring in nature. Given the prevalence of the various isotopes, the average of all of the atomic masses turns out to be 35.5 amu, which is slightly higher than chlorine's number on the periodic table. As another example, carbon has an atomic number of 12, but its atomic mass is 12.01 amu because, unlike chlorine, there are few naturally occurring isotopes to raise the average number.

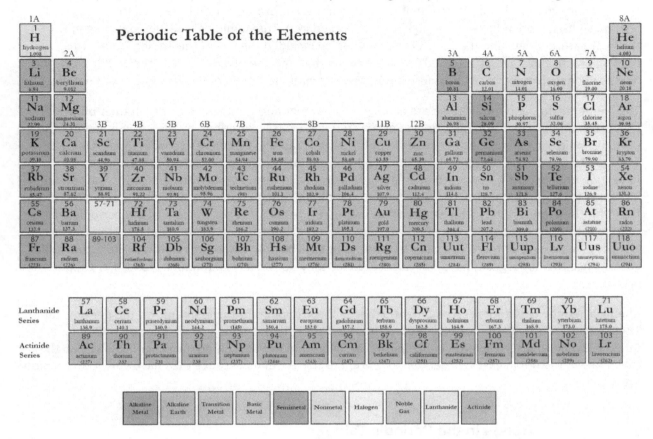

Periodic Table of the Elements

Elements are arranged according to their valance electron configurations, which also contribute to trends in chemical properties. These properties help to further categorize the elements into blocks, including metals, non-metals, transition metals, alkali metals, alkali earth metals, metalloids, lanthanides, actinides, diatomics, post-transition metals, polyatomic non-metals, and noble gases. Noble gases (the far-right column) have a full outer electron valence shell. The elements in this block possess similar characteristics such as being colorless, odorless, and having low chemical reactivity. Another block, the metals, tend to be shiny, highly conductive, and easily form alloys with each other, non-metals, and noble gases.

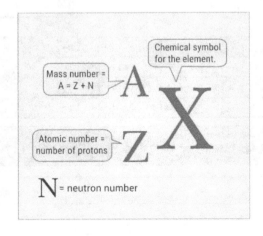

The symbols of the elements on the periodic table are a single letter or a two-letter combination that is usually derived from the element's name. Many of the elements have Latin origins for their names, and their atomic symbols do not match their modern names. For example, iron is derived from the word *ferrum*, so its symbol is Fe, even though it is now called iron. The naming of the elements began with those of natural origin and their ancient names, which included the use of the ending "ium." This naming practice has been continued for all elements that have been named since the 1940s. Now, the names of new elements must be approved by the International Union of Pure and Applied Chemistry.

The elements on the periodic table are arranged by number and grouped by trends in their physical properties and electron configurations. Certain trends are easily described by the arrangement of the periodic table, which includes the increase of the atomic radius as elements go from right to left and from top to bottom on the periodic table. Another trend on the periodic table is the increase in ionization energy (or the tendency of an atom to attract and form bonds with electrons). This tendency increases from left to right and from bottom to top of the periodic table—the opposite directions of the trend for the atomic radius. The elements on the right side and near the bottom of the periodic table tend to attract electrons with the intent to gain, while the elements on the left and near the top usually lose, or give up, one or more electrons in order to bond. The only exceptions to this rule are the noble gases. Since the noble gases have full valence shells, they do not have a tendency to lose or gain electrons.

Chemical reactivity is another trend identifiable by the groupings of the elements on the periodic table. The chemical reactivity of metals decreases from left to right and while going higher on the table. Conversely, non-metals increase in chemical reactivity from left to right and while going lower on the table. Again, the noble gases present an exception to these trends because they have very low chemical reactivity.

Trends in the Periodic Table

States of Matter and Factors that Affect Phase Changes

Matter is most commonly found in three distinct states: solid, liquid, and gas. A solid has a distinct shape and a defined volume. A liquid has a more loosely defined shape and a definite volume, while a gas has no definite shape or volume. The *Kinetic Theory of Matter* states that matter is composed of a large number of small particles (specifically, atoms and molecules) that are in constant motion. The distance between the separations in these particles determines the state of the matter: solid, liquid, or gas. In gases, the particles have a large separation and no attractive forces. In liquids, there is moderate separation between particles and some attractive forces to form a loose shape. Solids have almost no separation between their particles, causing a defined and set shape. The constant movement of particles causes them to bump into each other, thus allowing the particles to transfer energy between each other. This bumping and transferring of energy helps explain the transfer of heat and the relationship between pressure, volume, and temperature.

The *Ideal Gas Law* states that pressure, volume, and temperature are all related through the equation: $PV = nRT$, where P is pressure, V is volume, n is the amount of the substance in moles, R is the gas constant, and T is temperature.

Through this relationship, volume and pressure are both proportional to temperature, but pressure is inversely proportional to volume. Therefore, if the equation is balanced, and the volume decreases in the system, pressure needs to proportionately increase to keep both sides of the equation balanced. In contrast, if the equation is unbalanced and the pressure increases, then the temperature would also increase, since pressure and temperature are directly proportional.

When pressure, temperature, or volume change in matter, a change in state can occur. Changes in state include solid to liquid (melting), liquid to gas (evaporation), solid to gas (sublimation), gas to solid (deposition), gas to liquid (condensation), and liquid to solid (freezing). There is one other state of matter called *plasma*, which is seen in lightning, television screens, and neon lights. Plasma is most commonly converted from the gas state at extremely high temperatures.

The amount of energy needed to change matter from one state to another is labeled by the terms for phase changes. For example, the temperature needed to supply enough energy for matter to change from a liquid to a gas is called the *heat of vaporization*. When heat is added to matter in order to cause a change in state, there will be an increase in temperature until the matter is about to change its state. During its transition, all of the added heat is used by the matter to change its state, so there is no increase in temperature. Once the transition is complete, then the added heat will again yield an increase in temperature.

Each state of matter is considered to be a phase, and changes between phases are represented by phase diagrams. These diagrams show the effects of changes in pressure and temperature on matter. The states of matter fall into areas on these charts called *heating curves*.

Chemical Nomenclature, Composition, and Bonding

Simple Compounds and Their Chemical Formulas

Chemical formulas represent the proportion of the number of atoms in a chemical compound. Chemical symbols are used for the elements present and numerical values. Parentheses are also sometimes used to show the number of combinations of the elements in relation to their ionic charges. An element's ionic charge can be determined by its location on the periodic table. This information is then used to correctly combine its atoms in a compound.

For example, the chemical formula for sodium chloride (table salt) is the combination of sodium (Na, ionic charge of +1) and chlorine (Cl, ionic charge of -1). From its placement on the periodic table, the electron valence of an outer shell can be determined: sodium has an ionic charge of +1, while chlorine has an ionic charge of -1. Since these two elements have an equal and opposite amount of charge, they combine in a neutral one-to-one ratio: NaCl. The naming of compounds depends mainly on the second element in a chemical compound. If it is a non-metal (such as chlorine), it is written with an "ide" at the end. The compound NaCl is called "sodium chloride."

If the elements forming a compound do not have equal and opposite ionic charges, there will be an unequal number of each element in the compound to balance the ionic charge. This situation happens with many elements, for example, in the combination of nickel and oxygen into nickel oxide (Ni_2O_3). Nickel has a +3 ionic charge and oxygen has a -2 ionic charge, so when forming a compound, there must be two nickel atoms for every three oxygen atoms (a common factor of 6) to balance the charge of the compound. This compound is called "nickel oxide."

A chemical formula can also be written from a compound's name. For instance, the compound carbon dioxide is formed by the combination of carbon and oxygen. The word "dioxide" means there are two oxygen atoms for every carbon atom, so it is written as CO_2.

To better represent the composition of compounds, structural formulas are used. The combination of atoms is more precisely depicted by lining up the electron configuration of the outer electron shell through a Lewis dot diagram.

The Lewis dot diagram, named for Gilbert N. Lewis, shows the arrangement of the electrons in the outer shell and how these electrons can pair/bond with the outer shell electrons of other atoms when forming compounds. The diagram is created by writing the symbol of an element and then drawing dots to represent the outer shell of valence electrons around what would be an invisible square surrounding the symbol. The placement of the first two dots can vary based on the school of teaching. For the given example, the first dot is placed on the top and then the next dot is placed beside it, since it represents the pair of electrons in the 1s valence shell. The next dots (electrons) are placed one at a time on each side—right, bottom, left, right bottom left, etc.—of the element symbol until all of the valence shell electrons are represented, or the structure has eight dots (electrons), which means it is full. This method gives a more specific picture of compounds, how they are structured, and what electrons are available for bonding, sharing, and forming new compounds. For example, the compound sodium chloride is written separately with sodium having one valence electron and chlorine having seven valence electrons. Then, combined with a total of eight electrons, it is written with two dots being shared between the two elements.

Lewis structure NaCl

$$Na \cdot \ + \ \cdot \ddot{\underset{\cdot\cdot}{Cl}}: \ \longrightarrow \ Na^+ + \ :\ddot{\underset{\cdot\cdot}{Cl}}:^-$$

Types of Chemical Bonding

A chemical bond is a strong attractive force that can exist between atoms. The bonding of atoms is separated into two main categories. The first category, *ionic bonding,* primarily describes the bonding that occurs between oppositely charged ions in a regular crystal arrangement. It primarily exists between salts, which are known to be ionic. Ionic bonds are held together by the electrostatic attraction between oppositely charged ions. This type of bonding involves the transfer of electrons from the valence shell of one atom to the valence shell of another atom. If an atom loses an electron from its valence shell, it becomes a positive ion, or *cation*. If an atom gains an electron, it becomes a negative ion, or an *anion*. The Lewis electron-dot symbol is used to more simply express the electron configuration of atoms, especially when forming bonds.

The second type of bonding is covalent bonding. This bonding involves the sharing of a pair of electrons between atoms. There are no ions involved in covalent bonding, but the force holding the atoms together comes from the balance between the attractive and repulsive forces involving the shared electron and the nuclei. Atoms frequently engage is this type of bonding when it enables them to fill their outer valence shell.

Mole Concept and Its Applications

The calculation of mole ratios of reactants and products involved in a chemical reaction is called "stoichiometry." To find these ratios, one must first find the proportion of the number of molecules in one mole of a substance. This relates the molar mass of a compound to its mass and this relationship is a constant known as *Avogadro's number* (6.23×10^{23}). Since it is a ratio, there are no dimensions (or units) for Avogadro's number.

Molar Mass and Percent Composition

The molar mass of a substance is the measure of the mass of one mole of the substance. For pure elements, the molar mass is also known as the atomic mass unit (amu) of the substance. For compounds, it can be calculated by adding the molar masses of each substance in the compound. For example, the molar mass of carbon is 12.01 g/mol, while the molar mass of water (H_2O) requires finding the sum of the molar masses of the constituents ((1.01 x 2 = 2.02 g/mol for hydrogen) + (16.0 g/mol for oxygen) = 18.02 g/mol).

The percentage of a compound in a composition can be determined by taking the individual molar masses of each component divided by the total molar mass of the compound, multiplied by 100. Determining the percent composition of carbon dioxide (CO_2) first requires the calculation of the molar mass of CO_2.

molar mass of carbon = 12.01 x 1 atom = 12.01 g/mol

molar mass of oxygen = 16.0 × 2 atoms = 32.0 g/mol

molar mass of CO_2 = 12.01 g/mol + 32.0 g/mol = 44.01 g/mol

Next, each individual mass is divided by the total mass and multiplied by 100 to get the percent composition of each component.

12.01/44.01 = (0.2729 × 100) = 27.29% carbon

32.0/44.01 = (0.7271 × 100) = 72.71% oxygen

(A quick check in the addition of the percentages should always yield 100%.)

Chemical Reactions

Basic Concepts of Chemical Reactions

Chemical reactions rearrange the initial atoms of the reactants into different substances. These types of reactions can be expressed through the use of balanced chemical equations. A *chemical equation* is the symbolic representation of a chemical reaction through the use of chemical terms. The reactants at the beginning (or on the left side) of the equation must equal the products at the end (or on the right side) of the equation.

For example, table salt (NaCl) forms through the chemical reaction between sodium (Na) and chlorine (Cl) and is written as: $Na + Cl_2 \rightarrow NaCl$.

However, this equation is not balanced because there are two sodium atoms for every pair of chlorine atoms involved in this reaction. So, the left side is written as: $2Na + Cl_2 \rightarrow NaCl$.

Next, the right side needs to balance the same number of sodium and chlorine atoms. So, the right side is written as: $2Na + Cl_2 \rightarrow 2NaCl$. Now, this is a balanced chemical equation.

Chemical reactions typically fall into two types of categories: *endothermic* and *exothermic*.

An endothermic reaction absorbs heat, whereas an exothermic reaction releases heat. For example, in an endothermic reaction, heat is drawn from the container holding the chemicals, which cools the container. Conversely, an exothermic reaction emits heat from the reaction and warms the container holding the chemicals.

Factors that can affect the rate of a reaction include temperature, pressure, the physical state of the reactants (e.g., surface area), concentration, and catalysts/enzymes.

The formula $PV = nRT$ shows that an increase in any of the variables (pressure, volume, or temperature) affects the overall reaction. The physical state of two reactants can also determine how much interaction they have with each other. If two reactants are both in a fluid state, they may have the capability of interacting more than if solid. The addition of a catalyst or an enzyme can increase the rate of a chemical reaction, without the catalyst or enzyme undergoing a change itself.

Le Chatelier's principle describes factors that affect a reaction's equilibrium. Essentially, when introducing a "shock" to a system (or chemical reaction), a positive feedback/shift in equilibrium is often the response. In accordance with the second law of thermodynamics, this imbalance will eventually even itself out, but not without counteracting the effects of the reaction.

There are many different types of chemical reactions. A *synthesis reaction* is the combination of two or more elements into a compound. For example, the synthesis reaction of hydrogen and oxygen forms water.

$$2 H_2(g) + O_2(g) \rightarrow 2 H_2O(g)$$

A *decomposition reaction* is the breaking down of a compound into its more basic components. For example, the decomposition, or electrolysis, of water results in it breaking down into oxygen and hydrogen gas.

$$2 H_2O \rightarrow 2 H_2 + O_2$$

A *combustion reaction* is similar to a decomposition reaction, but it requires oxygen and heat for the reaction to occur. For example, the burning of a candle requires oxygen to ignite and the reaction forms carbon dioxide during the process.

$$CH_4(g) + 2O_2(g) \rightarrow CO_2(g) + 2H_2O(g)$$

There are also single and double replacement reactions where compounds swap components with each other to form new compounds. In the *single replacement reaction*, a single element will swap into a compound, thus releasing one of the compound's elements to become the new single element. For example, the reaction between iron and copper sulfate will create copper and iron sulfate.

$$1Fe(s) + 1CuSO_4(aq) \rightarrow 1FeSO_4(aq) + 1Cu(s)$$

In a *double replacement reaction*, two compounds swap components to form two new compounds. For example, the reaction between sodium sulfide and hydrochloric acid forms sodium chloride and hydrogen sulfide.

$$Na2S + HCl \rightarrow NaCl + H2S$$

After balancing the reaction, we get:

$$Na2S + 2HCl \rightarrow 2NaCl + H2S$$

An organic reaction is a chemical reaction involving the components of carbon and hydrogen.

Finally, there are oxidation/reduction (redox or half) reactions. These reactions involve the loss of electrons from one species (oxidation), and the gain of electrons to the other species (reduction). For example, the oxidation of magnesium is as follows:

$$2 Mg(s) + O_2(g) \rightarrow 2 MgO(s)$$

Acid-Base Chemistry

Simple Acid-Base Chemistry
If something has a sour taste, it is acidic, and if something has a bitter taste, it is basic. Unfortunately, it can be extremely dangerous to ingest chemicals in an attempt to classify them as an acid or a base. Therefore, acids and bases are generally identified by the reactions they have when combined with water. An acid will increase the concentration of the hydrogen ion (H^+), while a base will increase the concentration of the hydroxide ion (OH^-).

To better categorize the varying strengths of acids and bases, the pH scale is used. The pH scale provides a logarithmic (base 10) grading to acids and bases based on their strength. The pH scale contains values from 0 through 14, with 7 being neutral. If a solution registers below 7 on the pH scale, it is considered an acid. If it registers higher than 7, it is considered a base. To perform a quick test on a solution, litmus paper can be used. A base will turn red litmus paper blue, whereas an acid will turn blue litmus paper red. To gauge the strength of an acid or base, a test of phenolphthalein can be used. An acid will turn red phenolphthalein colorless, and a base will turn colorless phenolphthalein pink. As demonstrated with these types of tests, acids and bases neutralize each other. When acids and bases react with one another, they produce salts (also called ionic substances).

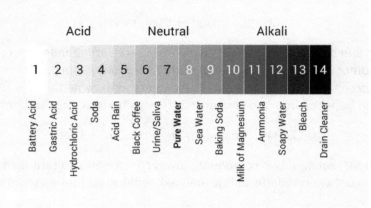

Solutions and Solubility

Different Types of Solutions

A *solution* is a homogenous mixture of more than one substance. A *solute* is another substance that can be dissolved into a substance called a *solvent*. If only a small amount of solute is dissolved in a solvent, the solution formed is said to be *diluted*. If a large amount of solute is dissolved into the solvent, then the solution is said to be *concentrated*. For example, water from a typical, unfiltered household tap is diluted because it contains other minerals in very small amounts.

Solution Concentration

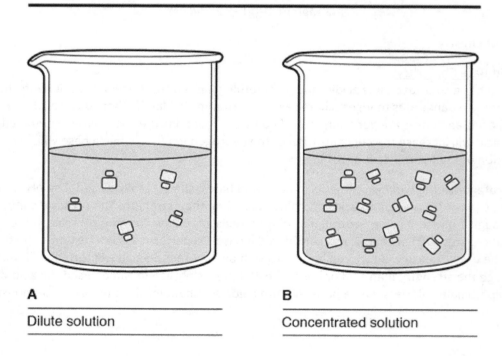

A
Dilute solution

B
Concentrated solution

If more solute is being added to a solvent, but not dissolving, the solution is called *saturated*. For example, when hummingbirds eat sugar-water from feeders, they prefer it as sweet as possible. When trying to dissolve enough sugar (solute) into the water (solvent), there will be a point where the sugar crystals will no longer dissolve into the solution and will remain as whole pieces floating in the water. At this point, the solution is considered saturated and cannot accept more sugar. This level, at which a solvent cannot accept and dissolve any more solute, is called its *saturation point*. In some cases, it is possible to force more solute to be dissolved into a solvent, but this will result in crystallization. The state of a solution on the verge of crystallization, or in the process of crystallization, is called a *supersaturated* solution. This can also occur in a solution that seems stable, but if it is disturbed, the change can begin the crystallization process.

Although the terms *dilute*, *concentrated*, *saturated*, and *supersaturated* give qualitative descriptions of solutions, a more precise quantitative description needs to be established for the use of chemicals. This holds true especially for mixing strong acids or bases. The method for calculating the concentration of a solution is done through finding its molarity. In some instances, such as environmental reporting, molarity is measured in parts per million (ppm). Parts per million, is the number of milligrams of a substance dissolved in one liter of water. To find the *molarity*, or the amount of solute per unit volume of solution, for a solution, the following formula is used:

$$c = \frac{n}{V}$$

In this formula, *c* is the molarity (or unit moles of solute per volume of solution), *n* is the amount of solute measured in moles, and *V* is the volume of the solution, measured in liters.

Example:

What is the molarity of a solution made by dissolving 2.0 grams of NaCl into enough water to make 100 mL of solution?

To solve this, the number of moles of NaCl needs to be calculated:

First, to find the mass of NaCl, the mass of each of the molecule's atoms is added together as follows:

23.0g (Na) + 35.5g (Cl) = 58.8g NaCl

Next, the given mass of the substance is multiplied by one mole per total mass of the substance:

2.0g NaCl × (1 mol NaCl/58.5g NaCl) = 0.034 mol NaCl

Finally, the moles are divided by the number of liters of the solution to find the molarity:

(0.034 mol NaCl)/(0.100L) = 0.34 M NaCl

To prepare a solution of a different concentration, the *mass solute* must be calculated from the molarity of the solution. This is done via the following process:

Example:

How would you prepare 600.0 mL of 1.20 M solution of sodium chloride?

To solve this, the given information needs to be set up:

$$1.20 \text{ M NaCl} = 1.20 \text{ mol NaCl}/1.00 \text{ L of solution}$$

$$0.600 \text{ L solution} \times (1.20 \text{ mol NaCl}/1.00 \text{ L of solution}) = 0.72 \text{ moles NaCl}$$

$$0.72 \text{ moles NaCl} \times (58.5\text{g NaCl}/1 \text{ mol NaCl}) = 42.12 \text{ g NaCl}$$

This means that one must dissolve 42.12 g NaCl in enough water to make 600.0 L of solution.

Factors Affecting the Solubility of Substances and the Dissolving Process
Certain factors can affect the rate in dissolving processes. These include temperature, pressure, particle size, and agitation (stirring). As mentioned, the *ideal gas law* states that $PV = nRT$, where P equals pressure, V equals volume, and T equals temperature. If the pressure, volume, or temperature are affected in a system, it will affect the entire system. Specifically, if there is an increase in temperature, there will be an increase in the dissolving rate. An increase in the pressure can also increase the dissolving rate. Particle size and agitation can also influence the dissolving rate, since all of these factors contribute to the breaking of intermolecular forces that hold solute particles together. Once these forces are broken, the solute particles can link to particles in the solvent, thus dissolving the solute.

A *solubility curve* shows the relationship between the mass of solute that a solvent holds at a given temperature. If a reading is on the solubility curve, the solvent is *full* (*saturated*) and cannot hold anymore solute. If a reading is above the curve, the solvent is *unstable* (*supersaturated*) from holding more solute than it should. If a reading is below the curve, the solvent is *unsaturated* and could hold more solute.

If a solvent has different electronegativities, or partial charges, it is considered to be *polar*. Water is an example of a polar solvent. If a solvent has similar electronegativities, or lacking partial charges, it is considered to be *non-polar*. Benzene is an example of a non-polar solvent. Polarity status is important when attempting to dissolve solutes. The phrase "like dissolves like" is the key to remembering what will happen when attempting to dissolve a solute in a solvent. A polar solute will dissolve in a like, or polar solvent. Similarly, a non-polar solute will dissolve in a non-polar solvent. When a reaction produces a solid, the solid is called a *precipitate.* A precipitation reaction can be used for removing a salt (an ionic compound that results from a neutralization reaction) from a solvent, such as water. For water, this process is called *ionization*. Therefore, the products of a neutralization reaction (when an acid and base react) are a salt and water.

When a solute is added to a solvent to lower the freezing point of the solvent, it is called *freezing point depression*. This is a useful process, especially when applied in colder temperatures. For example, the addition of salt to ice in winter allows the ice to melt at a much lower temperature, thus creating safer road conditions for driving. Unfortunately, the freezing point depression from salt can only lower the melting point of ice so far and is ineffectual when temperatures are too low. This same process, with a mix of ethylene glycol and water, is also used to keep the radiator fluid (antifreeze) in an automobile from freezing during the winter.

Physics

Mechanics

Description of Motion in One and Two Dimensions

The description of motion is known as *kinetics*, and the causes of motion are known as *dynamics*. Motion in one dimension is known as a *scalar* quantity. It consists of one measurement such as length (length or distance is also known as displacement), speed, or time. Motion in two dimensions is known as a *vector* quantity. This would be a speed with a direction, or velocity.

Velocity is the measure of the change in distance over the change in time. All vector quantities have a direction that can be relayed through the sign of an answer, such as -5.0 m/s or +5.0 m/s. The objects registering these velocities would be in opposite directions, where the change in distance is denoted by Δx and the change in time is denoted by Δt:

$$v = \frac{\Delta x}{\Delta t}$$

Acceleration is the measure of the change in an object's velocity over a change in time, where the change in velocity, $v_2 - v_1$, is denoted by Δv and the change in time, $t_1 - t_2$, is denoted by Δt:

$$a = \frac{\Delta v}{\Delta t}$$

The linear momentum, p, of an object is the result of the objects mass, m, multiplied by its velocity, v, and is described by the equation:

$$p = mv$$

This aspect becomes important when one object hits another object. For example, the linear momentum of a small sports car will be much smaller than the linear momentum of a large semi-truck. Thus, the semi-truck will cause more damage to the car than the car to the truck.

Newton's Three Laws of Motion

Sir Isaac Newton summarized his observations and calculations relating to motion into three concise laws.

First Law of Motion: Inertia

This law states that an object in motion tends to stay in motion or an object at rest tends to stay at rest, unless the object is acted upon by an outside force.

For example, a rock sitting on the ground will remain in the same place, unless it is pushed or lifted from its place.

The First Law also includes the relation of weight to gravity and force between objects relative to the distance separating them.

$$Weight = G\frac{Mm}{r^2}$$

In this equation, G is the gravitational constant, M and m are the masses of the two objects, and r is the distance separating the two objects.

Second Law of Motion: F = ma
This law states that the force on a given body is the result of the object's mass multiplied by any acceleration acting upon the object. For objects falling on Earth, an acceleration is caused by gravitational force ($9.8 \ m/s^2$).

Third Law of Motion: Action-Reaction
This law states that for every action there is an equal and opposite reaction. For example, if a person punches a wall, the wall exerts a force back on the person's hand equal and opposite to his or her punching force. Since the wall has more mass, it absorbs the impact of the punch better than the person's hand.

Mass, Weight, and Gravity
Mass is a measure of how much of a substance exists, or how much inertia an object has. The mass of an object does not change based on the object's location, but the weight of an object does vary with its location.

For example, a 15-kg mass has a weight that is determined by acceleration from the force of gravity here on Earth. However, if that same 15-kg mass were to be weighed on the moon, it would weigh much less, since the acceleration force from the moon's gravity is approximately one-sixth of that on Earth.

Weight = mass × acceleration

W_{Earth} = 15 kg × 9.8 m/s^2 > W_{Moon} = 15 kg × 1.62 m/s^2

W_{Earth} = 147N   >   24.3N

Analysis of Motion and Forces
Projectile Motion describes the path of an object in the air. Generally, it is described by two-dimensional movement, such as a stone thrown through the air. This activity maps to a parabolic curve. However, the definition of projectile motion also applies to free fall, or the non-arced motion of an object in a path straight up and/or straight down. When an object is thrown horizontally, it is subject to the same influence of gravity as an object that is dropped straight down. The farther the projectile motion, the farther the distance of the object's flight.

Friction is a force that opposes motion. It can be caused by a number of materials; there is even friction caused by air. Whenever two differing materials touch, rub, or pass by each other, it will create friction, or an oppositional force, unless the interaction occurs in a true vacuum. To move an object across a floor, the force exerted on the object must overcome the frictional force keeping the object in place. Friction is also why people can walk on surfaces. Without the oppositional force of friction to a shoe pressing on the floor, a person would not be able to grip the floor to walk—similar to the challenge of walking on ice. Without friction, shoes slip and are unable to help people propel forward and walk.

When calculating the effects of objects hitting (or colliding with) each other, several things are important to remember. One of these is the definition of momentum: the mass of an object multiplied by the object's velocity. As mentioned, it is expressed by the following equation:

$$p = mv$$

Here, p is equal to an object's momentum, m is equal to the object's mass, and v is equal to the object's velocity.

Another important thing to remember is the principle of the conservation of linear momentum. The total momentum for objects in a situation will be the same before and after a collision. There are two primary types of collisions: elastic and inelastic. In an elastic collision, the objects collide and then travel in different directions. During an inelastic collision, the objects collide and then stick together in their final direction of travel. The total momentum in an elastic collision is calculated by using the following formula:

$$m_1 v_1 + m_2 v_2 = m_1 v_1 + m_2 v_2$$

Here, m_1 and m_2 are the masses of two separate objects, and v_1 and v_2 are the velocities, respectively, of the two separate objects.

The total momentum in an inelastic collision is calculated by using the following formula:

$$m_1 v_1 + m_2 v_2 = (m_1 + m_2) v_f$$

Here, v_f is the final velocity of the two masses after they stick together post-collision.

Example:

If two bumper cars are speeding toward each other, head-on, and collide, they are designed to bounce off of each other and head in different directions. This would be an elastic collision.

If real cars are speeding toward each other, head-on, and collide, there is a good chance their bumpers might get caught together and their direction of travel would be together in the same direction.

An *axis* is an invisible line on which an object can rotate. This is most easily observed with a toy top. There is actually a point (or rod) through the center of the top on which the top can be observed to be spinning. This is called the axis.

When objects move in a circle by spinning on their own axis, or because they are tethered around a central point (also an axis), they exhibit circular motion. Circular motion is similar in many ways to linear (straight line) motion; however, there are a few additional points to note. A spinning object is always accelerating because it is always changing direction. The force causing this constant acceleration on or around an axis is called *centripetal force* and is often associated with centripetal acceleration. Centripetal force always pulls toward the axis of rotation. An imaginary reactionary force, called *centrifugal force*, is the outward force felt when an object is undergoing circular motion. This reactionary force is not the real force; it just feels like it is there. For this reason, it has also been referred to as a "fictional force." The true force is the one pulling inward, or the centripetal force.

The terms *centripetal* and *centrifugal* are often mistakenly interchanged. If the centripetal force acting on an object moving with circular motion is removed, the object will continue moving in a straight line tangent to the point on the circle where the object last experienced the centripetal force. For example, when a traditional style washing machine spins a load of clothes to expunge the water from the load, it rapidly spins the machine barrel. A force is pulling in toward the center of the circle (centripetal force). At the same time, the wet clothes, which are attempting to move in a straight line, are colliding with the outer wall of the barrel that is moving in a circle. The interaction between the wet clothes and barrel wall cause a reactionary force to the centripetal force and this expels the water out of the small holes that line the outer wall of the barrel.

Conservation of Angular Momentum

An object moving in a circular motion also has momentum; for circular motion, it is called *angular momentum*. This is determined by rotational inertia, rotational velocity, and the distance of the mass from the axis or center of rotation. When objects exhibit circular motion, they also demonstrate the *conservation of angular momentum*, meaning that the angular momentum of a system is always constant, regardless of the placement of the mass. Rotational inertia can be affected by how far the mass of the object is placed with respect to the axis of rotation. The greater the distance between the mass and the axis of rotation, the slower the rotational velocity. Conversely, if the mass is closer to the axis of rotation, the rotational velocity is faster. A change in one affects the other, thus conserving the angular momentum. This holds true as long as no external forces act upon the system.

For example, ice skaters spinning in on one ice skate extends their arms out for a slower rotational velocity. When skaters bring their arms in close to their bodies (which lessens the distance between the mass and the axis of rotation), their rotational velocity increases and they spin much faster. Some skaters extend their arms straight up above their head, which causes an extension of the axis of rotation, thus removing any distance between the mass and the center of rotation, which maximizes their rotational velocity.

Another example is when a person selects a horse on a merry-go-round: the placement of their horse can affect their ride experience. All of the horses are traveling with the same rotational speed, but in order to travel along the same plane as the merry-go-round turns, a horse on the outside will have a greater linear speed because it is further away from the axis of rotation. Essentially, an outer horse has to cover a lot more ground than a horse on the inside in order to keep up with the rotational speed of the merry-go-round platform. Thrill seekers should always select an outer horse.

The center of mass is the point that provides the average location for the total mass of a system. The word "system" can apply to just one object/particle or to many. The center of mass for a system can be calculated by finding the average of the mass of each object and multiplying by its distance from an origin point using the following formula:

$$x_{centerofmass} = \frac{m_1 x_1 + m_2 x_2}{m_1 + m_2}$$

In this case, *x* is the distance from the point of origin for the center of mass and each respective object, and *m* is the mass of each object.

To calculate for more than one object, the pattern can be continued by adding additional masses and their respective distances from the origin point.

Simple Machines

A simple machine is a mechanical device that changes the direction or magnitude of a force. There are six basic types of simple machines: lever, wedge, screw, inclined plane, wheel and axle, and pulley.

Here is how each type works and an example:

- A lever helps lift heavy items higher with less force, such as a crowbar lifting a large cast iron lid.

- A wedge helps apply force to a specific area by focusing the pressure, such as an axe splitting a tree.

- An inclined plane, such as a loading dock ramp, helps move heavy items up vertical distances with less force.

- A screw is an inclined plane wrapped around an axis and allows more force to be applied by extending the distance of the plane. For example, a screw being turned into a piece of wood provides greater securing strength than hitting a nail into the wood.

- A wheel and axle allows the use of rotational force around an axis to assist with applying force. For example, a wheelbarrow makes it easier to haul large loads by employing a wheel and axle at the front.

- A pulley is an application of a wheel and axle with the addition of cords or ropes and it helps move objects vertically. For example, pulling a bucket out of a well is easier with a pulley and ropes.

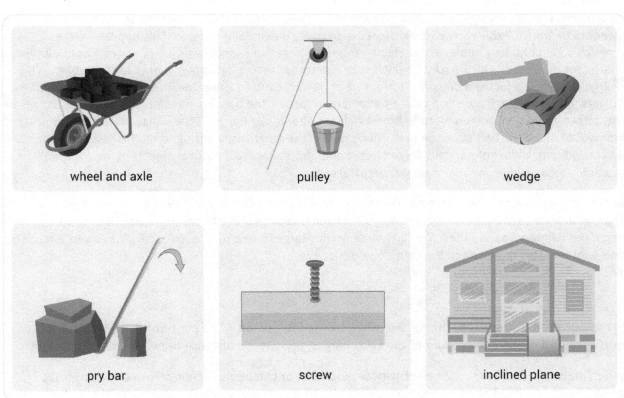

wheel and axle

pulley

wedge

pry bar

screw

inclined plane

Using a simple machine employs an advantage to the user. This is referred to as the mechanical advantage. It can be calculated by comparing the force input by the user to the simple machine with the force output from the use of the machine (also displayed as a ratio).

$$Mechanical\ Advantage\ = \frac{output\ force}{input\ force}$$

$$MA\ = \frac{F_{out}}{F_{in}}$$

In the following instance of using a lever, it can be helpful to calculate the torque, or circular force, necessary to move something. This is also employed when using a wrench to loosen a bolt.

$$Torque\ =\ F\ \times\ distance\ of\ lever\ arm\ from\ the\ axis\ of\ rotation\ (called\ the\ moment\ arm)$$

$$T\ =\ F\ \times\ d$$

Electricity and Magnetism

Electrical Nature of Common Materials
Generally, an atom carries no net charge because the positive charges of the protons in the nucleus balance the negative charges of the electrons in the outer shells of the atom. This is considered to be electrically neutral. However, since electrons are the only portion of the atom known to have the freedom to "move," this can cause an object to become electrically charged. This happens either through a gain or a loss of electrons. Electrons have a negative charge, so a gain creates a net negative charge for the object. On the contrary, a loss of electrons creates a positive charge for the object. This charge can also be focused on specific areas of an object, causing a notable interaction between charged objects. For example, if a person rubs a balloon on a carpet, the balloon transfers some of is electrons to the carpet. So, if that person were to hold a balloon near his or her hair, the electrons in the "neutral" hair would make the hair stand on end. This is due to the electrons wanting to fill the deficit of electrons on the balloon. Unless electrically forced into a charged state, most natural objects in nature tend toward reestablishing and maintaining a neutral charge.

When dealing with charges, it is easiest to remember that *like charges repel* each other and *opposite charges attract* each other. Therefore, negatives and positives attract, while two positives or two negatives will repel each other. Similarly, when two charges come near each other, they exert a force on one another. This is described through *Coulomb's Law*:

$$F\ =\ k\frac{q_1 q_2}{r^2}$$

In this equation, *F* is equal to the force exerted by the interaction, *k* is a constant (k = 8.99 x 10^9 N m²/C²), q_1 and q_2 are the measure of the two charges, and *r* is the distance between the two charges.

When materials readily transfer electricity or electrons, or can easily accept or lose electrons, they are considered to be good conductors. The transferring of electricity is called *conductivity*. If a material does not readily accept the transfer of electrons or readily loses electrons, it is considered to be an *insulator*. For example, copper wire easily transfers electricity because copper is a good conductor. However, plastic does not transfer electricity because it is not a good conductor. In fact, plastic is an insulator.

Basic Electrical Concepts

In an electrical circuit, the flow from a power source, or the voltage, is "drawn" across the components in the circuit from the positive end to the negative end. This flow of charge creates an electric current (*I*), which is the time (*t*) rate of flow of net charge (*q*). It is measured with the formula:

$$I = \frac{q}{t}$$

Current is measured in amperes (amps). There are two main types of currents:

1. *Direct current* (DC): a unidirectional flow of charges through a circuit

2. *Alternating current* (AC): a circuit with a changing directional flow of charges or magnitude

Every circuit will show a loss in voltage across its conducting material. This loss of voltage is from resistance within the circuit and can be caused by multiple factors, including resistance from wiring and components such as light bulbs and switches. To measure the resistance in a given circuit, Ohm's law is used:

$$Resistance = \frac{Voltage}{current} = R = \frac{V}{I}$$

Resistance (*R*) is measured in Ohms (Ω).

Components in a circuit can be wired *in series* or *in parallel*. If the components are wired in series, a single wire connects each component to the next in line. If the components are wired in parallel, two wires connect each component to the next. The main difference is that the voltage across those in series is directly related from one component to the next. Therefore, if the first component in the series becomes inoperable, no voltage can get to the other components. Conversely, the components in parallel share the voltage across each other and are not dependent on the prior component wired to allow the voltage across the wire.

To calculate the resistance of circuit components wired in series or parallel, the following equations are used:

Resistance in series:

$$R_{total} = R_1 + R_2 + R_3 + \cdots$$

Resistance in parallel:

$$R_{total} = \frac{1}{R_1} + \frac{1}{R_2} + \frac{1}{R_3} + \cdots$$

To make electrons move so that they can carry their charge, a change in voltage must be present. On a small scale, this is demonstrated through the electrons traveling from the light switch to a person's finger. This might happen in a situation where a person runs his or her socks on a carpet, touches a light switch, and receives a small jolt from the electrons that run from the switch to the finger. This minor jolt is due to the deficit of electrons created by rubbing the socks on the carpet, and then the electrons going into the ground. The difference in charge between the switch and the finger caused the electrons to move.

If this situation were to be created on a larger and more sustained scale, the factors would need to be more systematic, predictable, and harnessed. This could be achieved through batteries/cells and generators. Batteries or cells have a chemical reaction that occurs inside, causing energy to be released and charges to be able to move freely. Batteries generally have nodes (one positive and one negative), where items can be hooked up to complete a circuit and allow the charge to travel freely through the item. Generators convert mechanical energy into electric energy using power and movement.

Basic Properties of Magnetic Fields and Forces

Consider two straight rods that are made from magnetic material. They will naturally have a negative end (pole) and a positive end (pole). These charged poles react just like any charged item: opposite charges attract and like charges repel. They will attract each other when arranged positive pole to negative pole. However, if one rod is turned around, the two rods will now repel each other due to the alignment of negative to negative and positive to positive. These types of forces can also be created and amplified by using an electric current. For example, sending an electric current through a stretch of wire creates an electromagnetic force around the wire from the charge of the current. This force exists as long as the flow of electricity is sustained. This magnetic force can also attract and repel other items with magnetic properties. Depending on the strength of the current in the wire, a greater or smaller magnetic force can be generated around the wire. As soon as the current is stopped, the magnetic force also stops.

Optics and Waves

Electromagnetic Spectrum

The movement of light is described like the movement of waves. Light travels with a wave front, has an amplitude (height from the neutral), a cycle or wavelength, a period, and energy. Light travels at approximately 3.00×10^8 m/s and is faster than anything created by humans thus far.

Light is commonly referred to by its measured wavelengths, or the distance between two successive crests or troughs in a wave. Types of light with the longest wavelengths include radio, TV, and micro, and infrared waves. The next set of wavelengths are detectable by the human eye and create the *visible spectrum*. The visible spectrum has wavelengths of 10^{-7} m, and the colors seen are red, orange, yellow, green, blue, indigo, and violet. Beyond the visible spectrum are shorter wavelengths (also called the *electromagnetic spectrum*) containing ultraviolet light, X-rays, and gamma rays. The wavelengths outside of the visible light range can be harmful to humans if they are directly exposed or are exposed for long periods of time. For example, the light from the Sun has a small percentage of ultraviolet (UV) light, which is mostly absorbed by the UV layer of the Earth's atmosphere. When this layer does not filter out the UV rays, the exposure to the wavelengths can be harmful to humans' skin. When there is an extra layer of pollutants, and the light from the sun is trapped by repeated reflection to the Earth (so that it is unable to bounce back into space), it creates another harmful condition for the Earth called the *greenhouse effect*. This is an overexposure to the Sun's light and contributes to *global warming* by increasing the temperature on Earth.

Basic Characteristics and Types of Waves

A *mechanical wave* is a type of wave that passes through a medium (solid, liquid, or gas). There are two basic types of mechanical waves: longitudinal and transverse.

A *longitudinal wave* has motion that is parallel to the direction of the wave's travel. This can best be visualized by compressing one side of a tethered spring and then releasing that end. The movement travels in a bunching/un-bunching motion across the length of the spring and back.

A *transverse wave* has motion that is perpendicular to the direction of the wave's travel. The particles on a transverse wave do not move across the length of the wave; instead, they oscillate up and down, creating peaks and troughs.

A wave with a combination of both longitudinal and transverse motion can be seen through the motion of a wave on the ocean—with peaks and troughs, and particles oscillating up and down.

Mechanical waves can carry energy, sound, and light, but they need a medium through which transport can occur. An electromagnetic wave can transmit energy without a medium, or in a vacuum.

A more recent addition in the study of waves is the *gravitational wave*. Its existence has been proven and verified, yet the details surrounding its capabilities are still somewhat under inquiry. Gravitational waves are purported to be ripples that propagate as waves outward from their source and travel in the curvature of space/time. They are thought to carry energy in a form of radiant energy called *gravitational radiation*.

Basic Wave Phenomena
When a wave crosses a boundary or travels from one medium to another, certain things occur. If the wave can travel through one medium into another medium, it experiences *refraction*. This is the bending of the wave from one medium to another due to a change in density of the mediums, and thus, the speed of the wave changes. For example, when a pencil is sitting in half of a glass of water, a side view of the glass makes the pencil appear to be bent at the water level. What the viewer is seeing is the refraction of light waves traveling from the air into the water. Since the wave speed is slowed in water, the change makes the pencil appear bent.

When a wave hits a medium that it cannot penetrate, it is bounced back in an action called *reflection*. For example, when light waves hit a mirror, they are reflected, or bounced, off the mirror. This can cause it to seem like there is more light in the room, since there is a "doubling back" of the initial wave. This same phenomenon also causes people to be able to see their reflection in a mirror.

When a wave travels through a slit or around an obstacle, it is known as *diffraction*. A light wave will bend around an obstacle or through a slit and cause what is called a *diffraction pattern*. When the waves bend around an obstacle, it causes the addition of waves and the spreading of light on the other side of the opening.

Dispersion is used to describe the splitting of a single wave by refracting its components into separate parts. For example, if a wave of white light is sent through a dispersion prism, the light appears as its separate rainbow-colored components, due to each colored wavelength being refracted in the prism.

When wavelengths hit boundaries, different things occur. Objects will absorb certain wavelengths of light and reflect others, depending on the boundaries. This becomes important when an object appears to be a certain color. The color of an object is not actually within that object, but rather, in the wavelengths being transmitted by that object. For example, if a table appears to be red, that means the table is absorbing all other wavelengths of visible light except those of the red wavelength. The table is reflecting, or transmitting, the wavelengths associated with red back to the human eye, and so it appears red.

Interference describes when an object affects the path of a wave, or another wave interacts with a wave. Waves interacting with each other can result in either *constructive interference* or *destructive interference*, based on their positions. With constructive interference, the waves are in sync with each other and combine to reinforce each other. In the case of deconstructive interference, the waves are out of sync and reduce the effect of each other to some degree. In *scattering*, the boundary can change the direction or energy of a wave, thus altering the entire wave. *Polarization* changes the oscillations of a wave and can alter its appearance in light waves. For example, polarized sunglasses remove the "glare" from sunlight by altering the oscillation pattern observed by the wearer.

When a wave hits a boundary and is completely reflected, or if it cannot escape from one medium to another, it is called *total internal reflection*. This effect can be seen in the diamonds with a brilliant cut. The angle cut on the sides of the diamond causes the light hitting the diamond to be completely reflected back inside the gem, making it appear brighter and more colorful than a diamond with different angles cut into its surface.

The *Doppler effect* applies to situations with both light and sound waves. The premise of the Doppler effect is that, based upon the relative position or movement of a source and an observer, waves can seem shorter or longer than they actually are. When the Doppler effect is noted with sound, it warps the noise being heard by the observer. This makes the pitch or frequency seem shorter or higher as the source is approaching, and then longer or lower as the source is getting farther away. The frequency/pitch of the source never actually changes, but the sound in respect to the observer makes it seem like the sound has changed. This can be observed when a siren passes by an observer on the road. The siren sounds much higher in pitch as it approaches the observer and then lower after it passes and is getting farther away.

The Doppler effect also applies to situations involving light waves. An observer in space would see light approaching as being shorter wavelengths than the light actually is, causing it to look blue. When the light wave gets farther away, the light would appear red because of the apparent elongation of the wavelength. This is called the *red-blue shift*.

Basic Optics
When reflecting light, a mirror can be used to observe a virtual (not real) image. A *plane mirror* is a piece of glass with a coating in the background to create a reflective surface. An image is what the human eye sees when light is reflected off the mirror in an unmagnified manner. If a *curved mirror* is used for reflection, the image seen will not be a true reflection. Instead, the image will either be enlarged or miniaturized compared to its actual size. Curved mirrors can also make the object appear closer or farther away than the actual distance the object is from the mirror.

Lenses can be used to refract or bend light to form images. Examples of lenses are the human eye, microscopes, and telescopes. The human eye interprets the refraction of light into images that humans understand to be actual size. *Microscopes* allow objects that are too small for the unaided human eye to be enlarged enough to be seen. *Telescopes* allow objects to be viewed that are too far away to be seen with the unaided eye. *Prisms* are pieces of glass that can have a wavelength of light enter one side and appear to be divided into its component wavelengths on the other side. This is due to the ability of the prism to slow certain wavelengths more than others.

Sound
Sound travels in waves and is the movement of vibrations through a medium. It can travel through air (gas), land, water, etc. For example, the noise a human hears in the air is the vibration of the waves as they reach the ear. The human brain translates the different frequencies (pitches) and intensities of the vibrations to determine what created the noise.

A tuning fork has a predetermined frequency because of the length and thickness of its tines. When struck, it allows vibrations between the two tines to move the air at a specific rate. This creates a specific tone, or note, for that size of tuning fork. The number of vibrations over time is also steady for that tuning fork and can be matched with a frequency. All pitches heard by the human ear are categorized by using frequency and are measured in Hertz (cycles per second).

The level of sound in the air is measured with sound level meters on a decibel (dB) scale. These meters respond to changes in air pressure caused by sound waves and measure sound intensity. One decibel is 1/10th of a *bel*, named after Alexander Graham Bell, the inventor of the telephone. The decibel scale is logarithmic, so it is measured in factors of 10. This means, for example, that a 10 dB increase on a sound meter equates to a 10-fold increase in sound intensity.

Practice Questions

1. What is the total mechanical energy of a system?
    a. The total potential energy
    b. The total kinetic energy
    c. Kinetic energy plus potential energy
    d. Kinetic energy minus potential energy

2. What does the Lewis Dot structure of an element represent?
    a. The outer electron valence shell population
    b. The inner electron valence shell population
    c. The positioning of the element's protons
    d. The positioning of the element's neutrons

3. What is the name of the scale used in sound level meters to measure the intensity of sound waves?
    a. Doppler
    b. Electron
    c. Watt
    d. Decibel

4. Which statement is true regarding electrostatic charges?
    a. Like charges attract.
    b. Like charges repel.
    c. Like charges are neutral.
    d. Like charges neither attract nor repel.

5. What is the name of this compound: CO?
    a. Carbonite oxide
    b. Carbonic dioxide
    c. Carbonic oxide
    d. Carbon monoxide

6. What is the molarity of a solution made by dissolving 4.0 grams of $NaCl$ into enough water to make 120 mL of solution? The atomic mass of Na is 23.0 g/mol and Cl is 35.5 g/mol.
    a. 0.34 M
    b. 0.57 M
    c. 0.034 M
    d. 0.057 M

7. Considering a gas in a closed system, at a constant volume, what will happen to the temperature if the pressure is increased?
    a. The temperature will stay the same
    b. The temperature will decrease
    c. The temperature will increase
    d. It cannot be determined with the information given

8. What is the current when a 3.0 V battery is wired across a lightbulb that has a resistance of 6.0 ohms?
    a. 0.5 A
    b. 18.0 A
    c. 0.5 J
    d. 18.0 J

9. According to Newton's Three Laws of Motion, which of the following is true?
    a. Two objects cannot exert a force on each other without touching.
    b. An object at rest has no inertia.
    c. The weight of an object is the same as the mass of the object.
    d. The weight of an object is equal to the mass of an object multiplied by gravity.

10. What is the chemical reaction when a compound is broken down into its elemental components called?
    a. A synthesis reaction
    b. A decomposition reaction
    c. An organic reaction
    d. An oxidation reaction

11. Which of the following is a balanced chemical equation?
    a. $Na + Cl_2 \rightarrow NaCl$
    b. $2Na + Cl_2 \rightarrow NaCl$
    c. $2Na + Cl_2 \rightarrow 2NaCl$
    d. $2Na + 2Cl_2 \rightarrow 2NaCl$

12. What effect changes the oscillations of a wave and can alter the appearance of light waves?
    a. Reflection
    b. Refraction
    c. Dispersion
    d. Polarization

13. A spinning ice skater who extends his or her arms horizontally to slow down is demonstrating which of the following?
    a. Conservation of angular momentum
    b. Conservation of mechanical energy
    c. Conservation of matter
    d. Conservation of mass

14. The Sun transferring heat to the Earth through space is an example of which of the following?
    a. Convection
    b. Conduction
    c. Induction
    d. Radiation

15. What is the acceleration of a vehicle starting from rest and reaching a velocity of 15 m/s in 5.0 s?
    a. 3.0 m/s
    b. 75 m/s
    c. 3.0 m/s^2
    d. 75 m/s^2

16. What is 45 °C converted to °F?
    a. 113 °F
    b. 135 °F
    c. 57 °F
    d. 88 °F

17. What is the force that opposes motion?
    a. Reactive force
    b. Responsive force
    c. Friction
    d. Momentum

18. What type of chemical reaction produces a salt?
    a. An oxidation reaction
    b. A neutralization reaction
    c. A synthesis reaction
    d. A decomposition reaction

19. What does the decibel scale measure the intensity of?
    a. Sound waves
    b. Light waves
    c. Ocean waves
    d. Gravitational waves

20. The Doppler effect applies to sound waves and light waves. In space, what is this effect called?
    a. Red-black shift
    b. Red-blue shift
    c. Blue-black shift
    d. Blue-blue shift

21. Car A (mass 100 kg) traveling at 5 m/s hits Car B (mass 110 kg) traveling at 8 m/s in a head-on collision. The bumpers hook together during the collision so that Car A and Car B travel together after the impact. What is their combined velocity after impact?
    a. 13.0 m/s
    b. 3.0 m/s
    c. 6.6 m/s
    d. 16.6 m/s

22. Circular motion occurs around what?
    a. The center of mass
    b. The center of matter
    c. An elliptical
    d. An axis

23. If a reading is above the curve on a solubility curve, the solvent is considered to be which of the following?
    a. Unsaturated
    b. Supersaturated
    c. Stable
    d. Saturated

24. How is mechanical advantage calculated?
    a. The force input divided by the force output
    b. The force input multiplied by the force output
    c. The force output divided by 100
    d. The force output divided by the force input

25. Which of the following is a vector quantity?
    a. Mass
    b. Length
    c. Velocity
    d. Speed

Answer Explanations

1. C: In any system, the total mechanical energy is the sum of the potential energy and the kinetic energy. Either value could be zero but it still must be included in the total. Choices A and B only give the total potential or kinetic energy, respectively. Choice D gives the difference in the kinetic and potential energy.

2. A: A Lewis Dot diagram shows the alignment of the valence (outer) shell electrons and how readily they can pair or bond with the valence shell electrons of other atoms to form a compound. Choice B is incorrect because the Lewis Dot structure aids in understanding how likely an atom is to bond or not bond with another atom, so the inner shell would add no relevance to understanding this likelihood. The positioning of protons and neutrons concerns the nucleus of the atom, which again would not lend information to the likelihood of bonding.

3. D: The decibel scale is used to measure the intensity of sound waves. The decibel scale is a ratio of a particular sound's intensity to a standard value. Since it is a logarithmic scale, it is measured by a factor of 10. Choice A is the name of the effect experienced by an observer of a moving wave; Choice B is a particle in an atom; and Choice C is a unit for measuring power.

4. B: For charges, *like charges repel* each other and *opposite charges attract* each other. Negatives and positives will attract, while two positive charges or two negative charges will repel each other. Charges have an effect on each other, so Choices C and D are incorrect.

5. D: The naming of compounds focuses on the second element in a chemical compound. Elements from the non-metal category are written with an "ide" at the end. The compound CO has one carbon and one oxygen, so it is called carbon monoxide. Choice B represents that there are two oxygen atoms, and Choices A and B incorrectly alter the name of the first element, which should remain as carbon.

6. B: To solve this, the number of moles of NaCl needs to be calculated:

First, to find the mass of NaCl, the mass of each of the molecule's atoms is added together as follows:

$$23.0g (Na) + 35.5g (Cl) = 58.8g\ NaCl$$

Next, the given mass of the substance is multiplied by one mole per total mass of the substance:

$$4.0g\ NaCl \times (1\ mol\ NaCl/58.5g\ NaCl) = 0.068\ mol\ NaCl$$

Finally, the moles are divided by the number of liters of the solution to find the molarity:

$$(0.068\ mol\ NaCl)/(0.120L) = 0.57\ M\ NaCl$$

Choice A incorporates a miscalculation for the molar mass of NaCl, and Choices C and D both incorporate a miscalculation by not converting mL into liters (L), so they are incorrect by a factor of 10.

7. C: According to the *ideal gas law* ($PV = nRT$), if volume is constant, the temperature is directly related to the pressure in a system. Therefore, if the pressure increases, the temperature will increase in direct proportion. Choice A would not be possible, since the system is closed and a change is occurring, so the temperature will change. Choice B incorrectly exhibits an inverse relationship between pressure and temperature, or $P = 1/T$. Choice *D* is incorrect because even without actual values for the variables, the relationship and proportions can be determined.

8. A: According to Ohm's Law: $V = IR$, so using the given variables: $3.0 \text{ V} = I \times 6.0 \text{ }\Omega$

Solving for I: $I = 3.0 \text{ V}/6.0 \text{ }\Omega = 0.5 \text{ A}$

Choice *B* incorporates a miscalculation in the equation by multiplying 3.0 V by 6.0 Ω, rather than dividing these values. Choices *C* and *D* are labeled with the wrong units; Joules measure energy, not current.

9. D: The weight of an object is equal to the mass of the object multiplied by gravity. According to Newton's Second Law of Motion, $F = m \times a$. Weight is the force resulting from a given situation, so the mass of the object needs to be multiplied by the acceleration of gravity on Earth: $W = m \times g$. Choice *A* is incorrect because, according to Newton's first law, all objects exert some force on each other, based on their distance from each other and their masses. This is seen in planets, which affect each other's paths and those of their moons. Choice *B* is incorrect because an object in motion or at rest can have inertia; inertia is the resistance of a physical object to change its state of motion. Choice *C* is incorrect because the mass of an object is a measurement of how much substance of there is to the object, while the weight is gravity's effect of the mass.

10. B: A decomposition reaction breaks down a compound into its constituent elemental components. Choice *A* is incorrect because a synthesis reaction joins two or more elements into a single compound. Choice *C*, an organic reaction, is not possible, since it needs carbon and hydrogen for a reaction. Choice *D*, oxidation/reduction (redox or half) reaction, is incorrect because it involves the loss of electrons from one species (oxidation) and the gain of electrons to the other species (reduction). There is no notation of this occurring within the given reaction, so it is not correct.

11. C:

$$2Na + Cl_2 \longrightarrow 2NaCl$$

The number of each element must be equal on both sides of the equation:

Choice *C* is the only correct option: $2Na + Cl_2 \rightarrow 2NaCl$

2 Na + 2 Cl does equal 2 Na + 2 Cl (the number of sodium atoms and chlorine atoms match)

Choice *A*: $Na + Cl_2 \rightarrow NaCl$

1 Na + 2 Cl does not equal 1 Na + 1 Cl (the number of chlorine atoms do not match)

Choice *B*: $2Na + Cl_2 \rightarrow NaCl$

2 Na + 2 Cl does not equal 1 Na + 1 Cl (neither the number of sodium atoms nor chlorine atoms match)

Choice *D*: $2Na + 2Cl_2 \rightarrow 2NaCl$

2 Na + 4 Cl does not equal 2 Na + 2 Cl (the number of chlorine atoms do not match)

12. D: Polarization changes the oscillations of a wave and can alter the appearance in light waves. For example, polarized sunglasses remove the "glare" from sunlight by altering the oscillation pattern observed by the wearer. Choice *A*, reflection, is the bouncing back of a wave, such as in a mirror; Choice

B is the bending of a wave as it travels from one medium to another, such as going from air to water; and Choice *C*, dispersion, is the spreading of a wave through a barrier or a prism.

13. A: An object moving in a circular motion also has momentum; it is called *angular momentum* and it is determined by the amount of rotational inertia, rotational velocity, and the distance of the mass from the axis of rotation. Objects exhibiting circular motion also demonstrate the conservation of angular momentum. This means that the angular momentum of a system is always constant, regardless of the placement of the mass. Rotational inertia can be affected by the distance of the mass of the object from the center of rotation (axis of rotation). The farther the mass is from the center of rotation, the slower the rotational velocity. While Choices *B*, *C*, and *D* are all conserved, none of them deal directly with circular motion, so they would not apply to the question.

14. D: Radiation can be transmitted through electromagnetic waves and needs no medium to travel; it can travel in a vacuum. This is how the Sun warms the Earth and it typically applies to large objects with great amounts of heat, or objects that have a large difference in their heat measurements. Choice *A*, convection, involves atoms or molecules traveling from areas of high concentration to those of low concentration and transferring energy or heat with them. Choice *B*, conduction, involves the touching or bumping of atoms or molecules to transfer energy or heat. Choice *C*, induction, deals with charges and does not apply to the transfer of energy or heat. Choices *A*, *B*, and *C* need a medium in which to travel, while radiation requires no medium.

15. C: Review the following:

$$a = \frac{\Delta v}{\Delta t}$$

$$a = \frac{15 - 0}{5 - 0}$$

$$a = \frac{15}{5}$$

$$= 3.0 \text{ m/s}^2$$

Choices *A* and *B* have the wrong units for acceleration; they are labeled with the units for velocity. Choices *B* and *D* integrate a miscalculation with the formula—multiplying, rather than dividing, 15 and 5.

16. A: Review the following conversion:

$$^{\circ}F = \frac{9}{5}(^{\circ}C) + 32$$

$$^{\circ}F = \frac{9}{5}(45) + 32$$

$$^{\circ}F = 113\ ^{\circ}F$$

Choices *B*, *C*, and *D* all incorporate a mistake in the order of operations necessary for this calculation: divide, multiply, and then add.

17. C: The force that opposes motion is called *friction*. It also provides the resistance necessary for walking, running, braking, etc. In order for something to slide down a ramp, it must be acted upon by a force stronger than that of friction. Choices *A* and *B* are not actual terms, and Choice *C* is the measure of mass multiplied by velocity ($p = mv$).

18. B: A solid produced during a reaction is called a *precipitate.* In a neutralization reaction, the products (an acid and a base) react to form a salt and water. Choice *A*, an oxidation reaction, involves the transfer of an electron. Choice *C*, a synthesis reaction, involves the joining of two molecules to form a single molecule. Choice *D*, a decomposition reaction, involves the separation of a molecule into two other molecules.

19. A: The intensity of sound is measured on the decibel scale. This scale is a ratio of a particular sound's intensity with respect to a standard value. It is a logarithmic scale, meaning it is measure by a factor of 10. Choice *B* is incorrect because light intensity is measured in candelas (cd). Choice *C*, ocean waves, are measured by their size, and Choice *D*, gravitational waves, are measured in energy disturbance.

20. B: An observer in space would see light approaching as being of shorter wavelengths than in actuality, causing it to seem blue. When the light wave gets farther away, it would appear red due to the apparent elongation of the wavelength. This is called the red-blue shift. The other choices are just fictional color combinations.

21. C: Using the equation for the conservation of momentum for an inelastic collision:

$$m_1 v_1 + m_2 v_2 = (m_1 + m_2) v_f$$

m_1 = 100 kg

m_2 = 110 kg

v_1 = 5 m/s

v_2 = 8 m/s

$(100 \times 5) + (110 \times 8) = (100 + 110) \times v_f$

$(500) + (880) = (210) \times v_f$

$1380 = 210 \times v_f$

$1380/210 = v_f$

v_f = 6.6 m/s

Choices *A*, *B,* and *D* are answers created from possible mathematical errors when calculating the results.

22. D: Circular motion occurs around an invisible line around which an object can rotate. This invisible line is called an axis. Choice *A*, center of mass, is the average location of an object's mass. Choice *B*, the center of matter, is not a real term. Choice *C*, elliptical, describes an elongated circle and is not a viable selection.

23. B: When a solution is on the verge of—or in the process of—crystallization, it is called a *supersaturated* solution. This can also occur in a solution that seems stable, but if it is disturbed, the change can begin the crystallization process. To display the relationship between the mass of a solute that a solvent holds and a given temperature, a *solubility curve* is used. If a reading is on the solubility curve, the solvent is *saturated*; it is full and cannot hold more solute. If a reading is above the curve, the solvent is *supersaturated* and unstable from holding more solute than it should. If a reading is below the curve, the solvent is *unsaturated* and could hold more solute. Choices *A*, *C*, and *D* are all stable, whereas Choice *B* is unstable.

24. D: The *mechanical advantage* is calculated by comparing the force input by the user to the simple machine with the force output from the use of the machine. This calculation is performed through a ratio:

$$Mechanical\ Advantage\ = \frac{output\ force}{input\ force}$$

$$MA\ = \frac{F_{out}}{F_{in}}$$

Choice *A*, the force input divided by the force output, is the reciprocal of the mechanical advantage. Choice *B* is an incorrect equation and would result in a force, not a ratio. Choice *C* is not used for any calculation.

25. C: Motion with one dimension or measurement is known as a *scalar quantity,* and includes things like such as length, speed, or time. Motion with two dimensions is known as a *vector quantity*. This would be a speed with a direction, or velocity. Choices *A*, *B*, and *C* (mass, length, speed) are all measurements of magnitudes—one-dimension scalar quantities.

Life Science

Basic Structure and Function of Cells and Their Organelles

Structure and Function of Cell Membranes

All cells are surrounded by a cell membrane that is formed from two layers of phospholipids. *Phospholipids* are two fatty acid chains connected to a glycerol molecule with a phosphate group. The membrane is amphiphilic because the fatty acid chains are hydrophobic and the phosphate group is hydrophilic. This creates a unique environment that protects the cell's inner contents while still allowing material to pass through the membrane. Because the outside of a cell, known as the *extracellular space*, and the inside of a cell, the *intercellular space*, are aqueous, the lipid bilayer forms with the two phospholipid heads facing the outside and the inside of the cell. This allows the phospholipids to interact with water; the fatty acid tails face the middle, so they can interact with each other and avoid water.

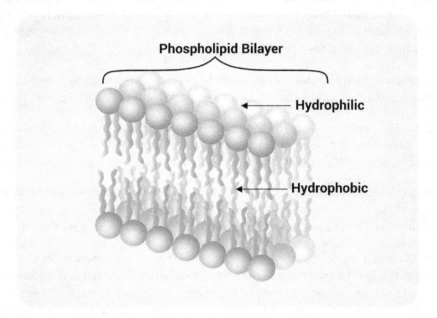

Molecules can pass through the cell membrane by either active or passive transport. *Active transport* requires chemical energy to move molecules in or out of the cell from areas of low concentration to areas of high concentration, or in instances where the molecules would not be able to pass through by themselves, such as with large non-lipid soluble molecules. Ions, amino acids, and complex sugars use active transport mechanisms. Molecules that are soluble in lipids, water, and oxygen use *passive transport* to move in and out of the cell, which means that cellular energy is not required for their movement. Examples of passive transport include diffusion, facilitated diffusion, and osmosis. *Diffusion* is the net movement of particles from an area of high concentration to lower concentration. *Facilitated diffusion* is the movement of molecules through cell membranes with the use of special transport proteins. Finally, *osmosis* is the movement of water molecules across partially permeable membranes.

Structure and Function of Animal and Plant Cell Organelles

Animal and plant cells contain many of the same or similar *organelles*, which are membrane enclosed structures that each have a specific function; however, there are a few organelles that are unique to either one or the other general cell type. The following cell organelles are found in both animal and plant cells, unless otherwise noted in their description:

- *Nucleus*: The nucleus consists of three parts: the nuclear envelope, the nucleolus, and chromatin. The *nuclear envelope* is the double membrane that surrounds the nucleus and separates its contents from the rest of the cell. The *nucleolus* produces ribosomes. *Chromatin* consists of DNA and protein, which form chromosomes that contain genetic information. Most cells have only one nucleus; however, some cells, such as skeletal muscle cells, have multiple nuclei.

- *Endoplasmic reticulum (ER)*: The ER is a network of membranous sacs and tubes that is responsible for membrane synthesis. It is also responsible for packaging and transporting proteins into vesicles that can move out of the cell. It folds and transports other proteins to the Golgi apparatus. It contains both smooth and rough regions; the rough regions have ribosomes attached, which are the sites of protein synthesis.

- *Flagellum*: Flagellum are found only in animal cells. They are made up of a cluster of microtubules projected out of the plasma membrane, and they aid in cell mobility.

- *Centrosome*: The centrosome is the area of the cell where *microtubules*, which are filaments that are responsible for movement in the cell, begin to be formed. Each centrosome contains two centrioles. Each cell contains one centrosome.

- *Cytoskeleton*: The cytoskeleton in animal cells is made up of microfilaments, intermediate filaments, and microtubules. In plant cells, the cytoskeleton is made up of only microfilaments and microtubules. These structures reinforce the cell's shape and aid in cell movement.

- *Microvilli*: Microvilli are found only in animal cells. They are protrusions in the cell membrane that increase the cell's surface area. They have a variety of functions, including absorption, secretion, and cellular adhesion. They are found on the apical surface of epithelial cells, such as in the small intestine. They are also located on the plasma surface of a female's eggs to help anchor sperm that are attempting fertilization.

- *Peroxisome*: A peroxisome contains enzymes that are involved in many of the cell's metabolic functions, one of the most important being the breakdown of very long chain fatty acids. Peroxisomes produces hydrogen peroxide as a byproduct of these processes and then converts the hydrogen peroxide to water. There are many peroxisomes in each cell.

- *Mitochondrion*: The mitochondrion is often called the powerhouse of the cell and is one of the most important structures for maintaining regular cell function. It is where aerobic cellular respiration occurs and where most of the cell's adenosine triphosphate (ATP) is generated. The number of mitochondria in a cell varies greatly from organism to organism, and from cell to cell. In human cells, the number of mitochondria can vary from zero in a red blood cell, to 2000 in a liver cell.

- *Lysosome*: Lysosomes are responsible for digestion and can hydrolyze macromolecules. There are many lysosomes in each cell.

- *Golgi apparatus*: The Golgi apparatus is responsible for the composition, modification, organization, and secretion of cell products. Because of its large size, it was actually one of the first organelles to be studied in detail. There are many Golgi apparati in each cell.

- *Ribosomes*: Ribosomes are found either free in the cytosol, bound to the rough ER, or bound to the nuclear envelope. They manufacture proteins within the cell.

- *Plasmodesmata*: The plasmodesmata are found only in plant cells. They are cytoplasmic channels, or tunnels, that go through the cell wall and connect the cytoplasm of adjacent cells.

- *Chloroplast*: Chloroplasts are found only in plant cells. They are responsible for *photosynthesis*, which is the process of converting sunlight to chemical energy that can be stored and used later to drive cellular activities.

- *Central vacuole*: A central vacuole is found only in plant cells. It is responsible for storing material and waste. This is the only vacuole found in a plant cell.

- *Plasma membrane*: The plasma membrane is a phospholipid bilayer that encloses the cell.

- *Cell wall*: Cell walls are only present in plant cells. The cell wall is made up of strong fibrous substances including cellulose and other polysaccharides, and protein. It is a layer outside of the plasma membrane, which protects the cell from mechanical damage and helps maintain the cell's shape.

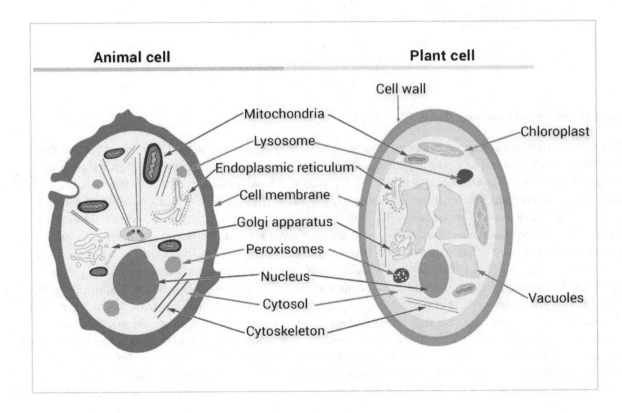

Levels of Organization

There are about two hundred different types of cells in the human body. Cells group together to form *biological tissues*, and tissues combine to form *organs*, such as the heart and kidneys. Organs that work together to perform vital functions of the human body form *organ systems*. There are eleven organ systems in the human body: skeletal, muscular, urinary, nervous, digestive, endocrine, reproductive, respiratory, cardiovascular, integumentary, and lymphatic. Although each system has its own unique function, they all rely on each other, either directly or indirectly, to operate properly.

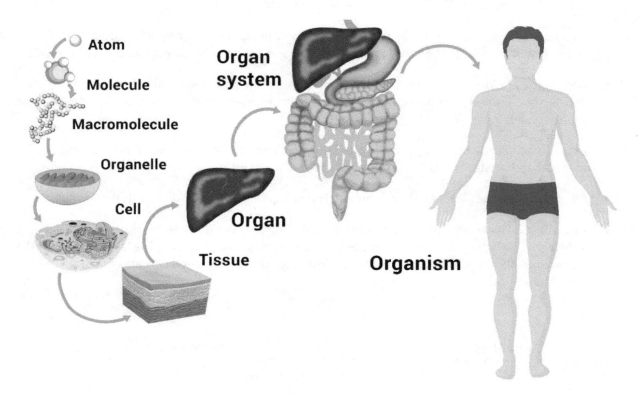

Major Features of Common Animal Cell Types

The most common animal cell types are blood, muscle, nerve, epithelial, and gamete cells. The three main blood cells are *red blood cells (RBCs), white blood cells (WBCs),* and *platelets*. RBCs transport oxygen and carbon dioxide through the body. They do not have a nucleus and they live for about 120 days in the blood. WBCs defend the body against diseases. They do have a nucleus and live for only three to four days in the human body. Platelets help with the formation of blood clots following an injury. They do not have a nucleus and live for about eight days after formation. *Muscle cells* are long, tubular cells that form muscles, which are responsible for movement in the body. On average, they live for about fifteen years, but this number is highly dependent on the individual body. There are three main types of muscle tissue: skeletal, cardiac, and smooth. *Skeletal muscle cells* have multiple nuclei and are the only voluntary muscle cell, which means that the brain consciously controls the movement of skeletal muscle. *Cardiac muscle cells* are only found in the heart; they have a single nucleus and are involuntary. *Smooth muscle cells* make up the walls of the blood vessels and organs. They have a single nucleus and are involuntary. *Nerve cells* conduct electrical impulses that help send information and instructions from the brain to the rest of the body. They contain a single nucleus and have a specialized membrane that allows for this electrical signaling between cells. *Epithelial* cells cover exposed surfaces, and line internal cavities and passageways. *Gametes* are specialized cells that are responsible for reproduction. In the human body, the gametes are the egg and the sperm.

Prokaryotes and Eukaryotes

There are two distinct types of cells that make up most living organisms: *prokaryotic* and *eukaryotic*. Both types of cells are enclosed by plasma membranes with cytosol on the inside. They both contain *ribosomes* and DNA. One major difference between these types of cells is that in eukaryotic cells, the cell's DNA is enclosed in a membrane-bound nucleus, whereas in prokaryotic cells, the cell's DNA is in a region—called the *nucleoid*—that is not enclosed by a membrane. Another major difference is that eukaryotic cells contain organelles, while prokaryotic cells do not have organelles.

Prokaryotic cells include *bacteria* and archaea. They do not have a nucleus or any membrane-bound organelles, are unicellular organisms, and are generally very small in size. Eukaryotic cells include animal, plant, fungus, and protist cells. *Fungi* are unicellular microorganisms such as yeasts, molds, and mushrooms. Their distinguishing characteristic is the chitin that is in their cell walls. *Protists* are organisms that are not classified as animals, plants, or fungi; they are unicellular; and they do not form tissues.

Key Aspects of Cell Reproduction and Division

Cell Cycle

The *cell cycle* is the process by which a cell divides and duplicates itself. There are two processes by which a cell can divide itself: mitosis and meiosis. In *mitosis*, the daughter cells that are produced from parental cell division are identical to each other and the parent. *Meiosis* is a unique process that involves two stages of cell division and produces *haploid cells*, which are cells containing only one set of chromosomes, from *diploid parent cells*, which are cells containing two sets of chromosomes.

The Cell Cycle

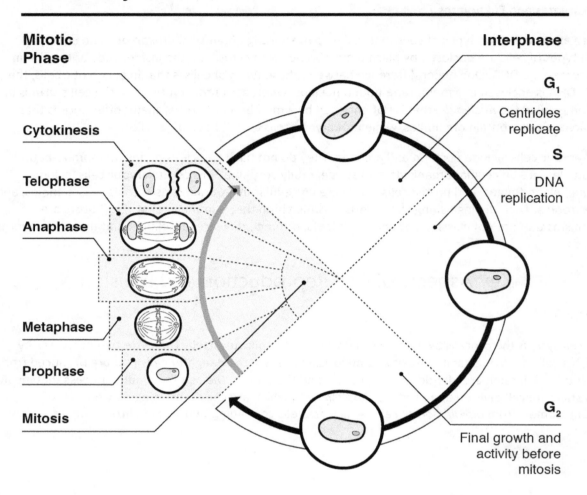

Mitosis

Mitosis can be broken down into five stages: prophase, prometaphase, metaphase, anaphase, and telophase.

- *Prophase*: During this phase, the mitotic spindles begin to form from centrosomes and microtubules. As the microtubules lengthen, the centrosomes move farther away from each other. The nucleolus disappears and the chromatin fibers begin to coil up and form chromosomes. Two sister chromatids, which are two copies of one chromosome, are joined together.

- *Prometaphase*: The nuclear envelope begins to break down and the microtubules enter the nuclear area. Each pair of chromatin fibers develops a *kinetochore*, which is a specialized protein structure in the middle of the adjoined fibers. The chromosomes are further condensed.

- *Metaphase*: In this stage, the microtubules are stretched across the cell and the centrosomes are at opposite ends of the cell. The chromosomes align at the *metaphase plate*, which is a plane that is exactly between the two centrosomes. The kinetochore of each chromosome is attached to the kinetochore of the microtubules that are stretching from each centrosome to the metaphase plate.

- *Anaphase*: The sister chromatids break apart, forming full-fledged chromosomes. The two daughter chromosomes move to opposite ends of the cell. The microtubules shorten toward opposite ends of the cell as well, and the cell elongates.

- *Telophase*: Two nuclei form at each end of the cell and nuclear envelopes begin to form around each nucleus. The nucleoli reappear and the chromosomes become less condensed. The microtubules are broken down by the cell and mitosis is complete.

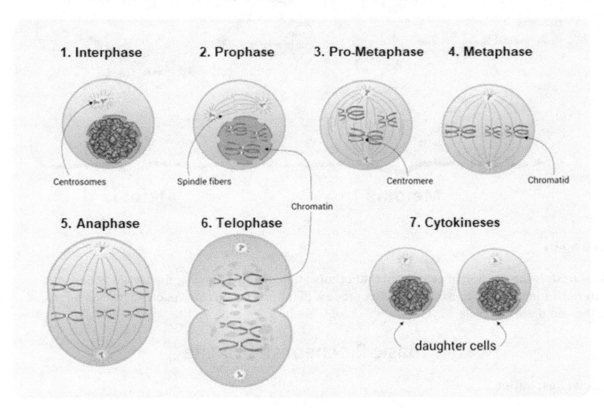

Meiosis

Meiosis is a type of cell division in which the daughter cells have half as many sets of chromosomes as the parent cell. In addition, one parent cell produces four daughter cells. Meiosis has the same phases as mitosis, except that they occur twice—once in meiosis I and once in meiosis II. The diploid parent has two sets of chromosomes, set A and set B. During meiosis I, each chromosome set duplicates, producing a second set of A chromosomes and a second set of B chromosomes, and the cell splits into two. Each cell contains two sets of chromosomes. Next, during meiosis II, the two intermediate daughter cells divide again, producing four total haploid cells that each contain one set of chromosomes. Two of the haploid cells each contain one chromosome of set A and the other two cells each contain one chromosome of set B.

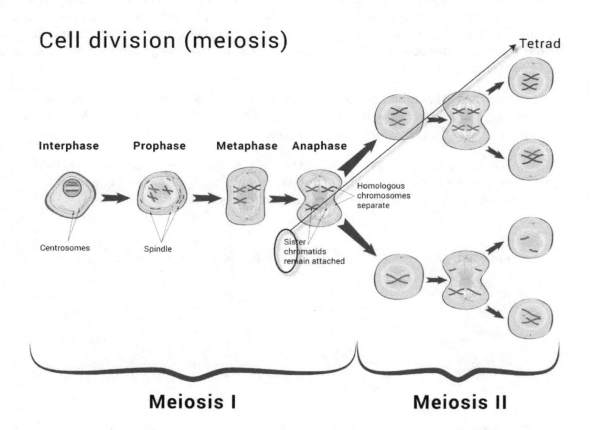

Cytokinesis

Cytokinesis is the division of cytoplasm that occurs immediately following the division of genetic material during cellular reproduction. The process of mitosis or meiosis, followed by cytokinesis, makes up the complete cell cycle.

Basic Biochemistry of Life

Cellular Respiration

Cellular respiration is a set of metabolic processes that converts energy from nutrients into ATP, which is the molecule of useable energy for the cell. Respiration can either occur aerobically, using oxygen, or anaerobically, without oxygen. While prokaryotic cells carry out respiration in the cytosol, most of the aerobic respiration in eukaryotic cells occurs in the mitochondria. Glycolysis and ATP-PC (phosphocreatine system) take place in the cytosol.

Anaerobic Respiration

Some organisms do not live in oxygen-rich environments and must find alternate methods of respiration. *Anaerobic respiration* occurs in certain prokaryotic organisms, and while it does occur in eukaryotic organisms, it happens in them much less frequently. The organisms utilize an electron transport chain similar to that of the aerobic respiration pathway; the terminal acceptor molecule, however, is an electronegative substance that is not an oxygen molecule. Some bacteria, for example, use the sulfate ion (SO_4^{2-}) as the final electron accepting molecule and the resulting byproduct is hydrogen sulfide (H_2S), instead of water.

Aerobic Respiration

There are two main steps in *aerobic cellular respiration*: the *citric acid cycle*, also known as the *Krebs cycle*, and *oxidative phosphorylation*. A process called *glycolysis* converts glucose molecules into pyruvate molecules and those pyruvate molecules then enter the citric acid cycle. The pyruvate molecules are broken down to produce ATP, as well as NADH and $FADH_2$—molecules that are used energetically to drive the next step of oxidative phosphorylation. During this phase of aerobic respiration, an electron transport chain pumps electrons and protons across the inner mitochondrial matrix. The electrons are accepted by an oxygen molecule, and water is produced. This process then fuels *chemiosmosis*, which helps convert ADP molecules to ATP. The total number of ATP molecules generated through aerobic respiration can be as many as thirty-eight, if none are lost during the process. Aerobic respiration is up to fifteen times more efficient than anaerobic respiration.

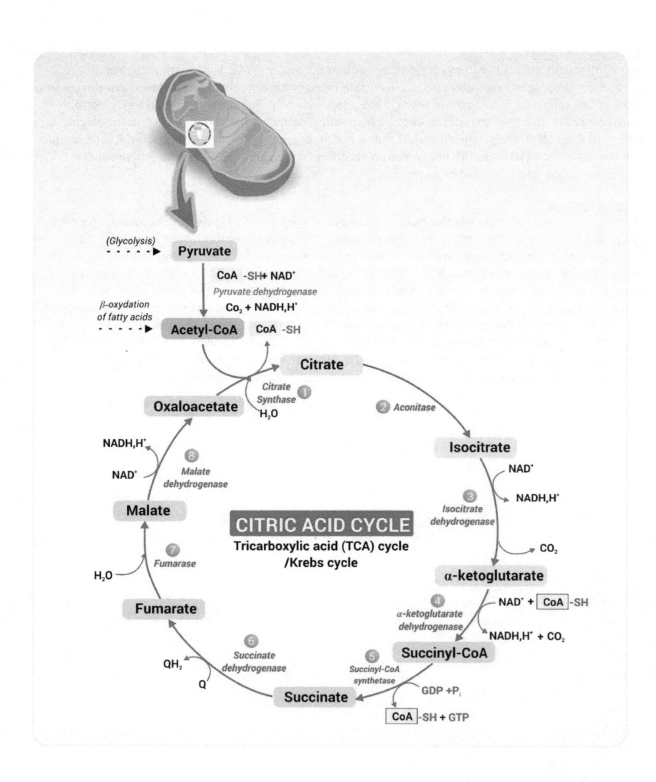

(Glycolysis) - - - - ▶ **Pyruvate**

β-oxydation
of fatty acids
- - - - ▶

CoA -SH+ NAD⁺
Pyruvate dehydrogenase
CO_2 + NADH,H⁺

Acetyl-CoA   CoA -SH

Citrate

Citrate Synthase ①   ② *Aconitase*
H_2O

Oxaloacetate

Isocitrate

NADH,H⁺

NAD⁺   *Malate dehydrogenase* ⑧

NAD⁺
③
NADH,H⁺
Isocitrate dehydrogenase
CO_2

Malate

CITRIC ACID CYCLE
Tricarboxylic acid (TCA) cycle /Krebs cycle

α-ketoglutarate

⑦ *Fumarase*
H_2O

④
α-ketoglutarate dehydrogenase
NAD⁺ + CoA -SH

NADH,H⁺ + CO_2

Fumarate

⑥
Succinate dehydrogenase   ⑤
Succinyl-CoA synthetase

Succinyl-CoA

QH_2

Q

Succinate   GDP +P_i

CoA -SH + GTP

Photosynthesis

Photosynthesis is the process of converting light energy into chemical energy, which is then stored in sugar and other organic molecules. It can be divided into two stages called the *light reactions* and the *Calvin cycle*. The photosynthetic process takes place in the chloroplast in plants. Inside the chloroplast, there are membranous sacs called *thylakoids*. *Chlorophyll* is a green pigment that lives in the thylakoid membranes, absorbs photons from light, and starts an electron transport chain in order to produce energy in the form of ATP and NADPH. The ATP and NADPH produced from the light reactions are used as energy to form organic molecules in the Calvin cycle.

The Calvin cycle takes place in the *stroma*, or inner space, of the chloroplasts. The process consumes nine ATP molecules and six NADPH molecules for every one molecule of glyceraldehyde 3-phosphate (G3P) that it produces. The G3P that is produced can be used as the starting material to build larger organic compounds, such as glucose. The complex series of reactions that takes place in photosynthesis can be simplified into the following equation: $6CO_2 + 12 H_2O + Light Energy \rightarrow C_6H_{12}O_6 + 6O_2 + 6H_2O$.

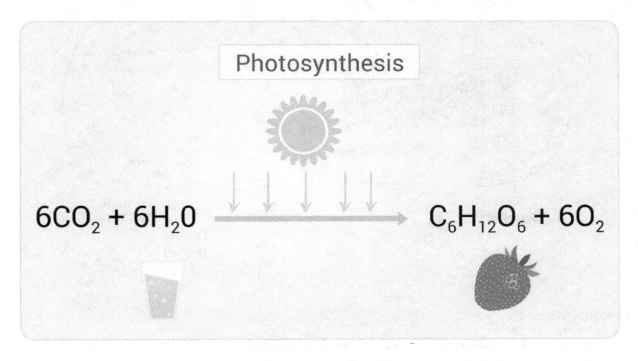

Basically, carbon dioxide and water mix with light energy inside the chloroplast to produce organic molecules, oxygen, and water. It is interesting to note that water is on both sides of the equation. Twelve water molecules are consumed during this process and six water molecules are newly formed as byproducts. Although the Calvin cycle itself is not dependent on light energy, both steps of photosynthesis usually occur during daylight because the Calvin cycle is dependent upon the ATP and NADPH that is produced by the light reactions.

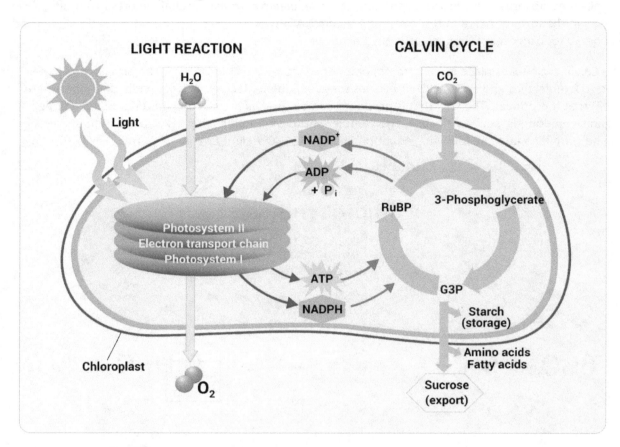

Biological Molecules

Repeating units of monomers (small molecules that bond with identical small molecules) that are linked together are called *polymers*. The most important polymers found in all living things can be divided into five categories: nucleic acids (such as DNA), carbohydrates, proteins, lipids, and enzymes. Carbon (C), hydrogen (H), oxygen (O), nitrogen (N), sulfur (S), and phosphorus (P) are the major elements of most biological molecules. Carbon is a common backbone of large molecules because of its ability to bond to four different atoms.

<u>DNA and RNA</u>
Nucleotides consist of a five-carbon sugar, a nitrogen-containing base, and one or more phosphate groups. *Deoxyribonucleic acid (DNA)* is made up of two strands of nucleotides coiled together in a double-helix structure. It plays a major role in enabling living organisms to pass their genetic information and complex components on to subsequent generations. There are four nitrogenous bases that make up DNA: adenine, thymine, guanine, and cytosine. Adenine always pairs with thymine, and guanine always

pairs with cytosine. *Ribonucleic acid (RNA)* is often made up of only one strand of nucleotides folded in on itself. Like DNA, RNA has four nitrogenous bases; however, in RNA, thymine is replaced by uracil.

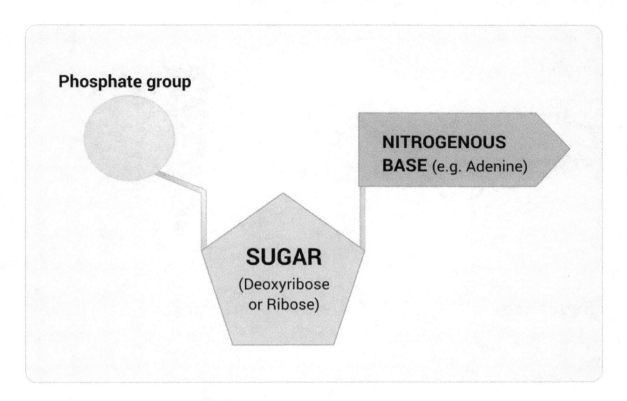

Carbohydrates

Carbohydrates consist of sugars and polymers of sugars, such as starches, which make up the cell walls of plants. The simplest sugar is called a *monosaccharide* and has the molecular formula of CH_2O, or a multiple of that formula. Monosaccharides are important molecules for cellular respiration. Their carbon skeleton can also be used to rebuild new small molecules. *Polysaccharides* are made up of a few hundred to a few thousand monosaccharides linked together.

Proteins

Proteins are essential for almost all functions in living beings. All proteins are made from a set of twenty *amino acids* that are linked in *unbranched polymers*. The amino acids are linked by *peptide bonds*, and polymers of amino acids are called *polypeptides*. These polypeptides, either individually or in linked combination with each other, fold up and form coils of biologically functional molecules.

There are four levels of protein structure: primary, secondary, tertiary, and quaternary. The *primary structure* is the sequence of amino acids, similar to the letters in a long word. The *secondary structure* comprises the folds and coils that are formed by hydrogen bonding between the slightly charged atoms of the polypeptide backbone. *Tertiary structure* is the overall shape of the molecule that results from the interactions between the side chains that are linked to the polypeptide backbone. *Quaternary structure* is the overall protein structure that occurs when a protein is made up of two or more polypeptide chains.

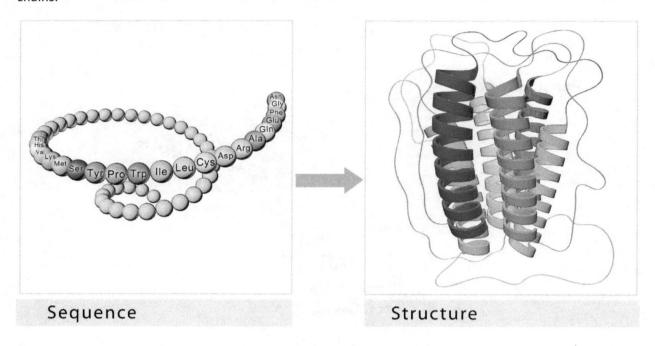

Sequence

Structure

Lipids

Lipids are a class of biological molecules that are *hydrophobic*, which means that they do not mix well with water. They are mostly made up of large chains of carbon and hydrogen atoms, termed *hydrocarbon chains*. The three most important types of lipids are fats, phospholipids, and steroids.

Fats are made up of two types of smaller molecules: three fatty acids and one glycerol molecule. Saturated fats do not have double bonds between the carbons in the fatty acid chain, such as glycerol, pictured below. They are fairly straight molecules and can pack together closely, so they form solids at room temperature. Unsaturated fats have one or more double bonds between carbons in the fatty acid chain. Since they cannot pack together as tightly as saturated fats, they take up more space and are called oils. They remain liquid at room temperature.

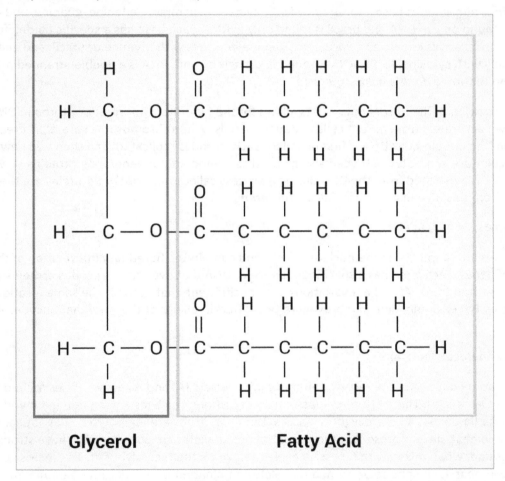

Glycerol   **Fatty Acid**

Phospholipids are made up of two fatty acid molecules linked to one glycerol molecule. When phospholipids are mixed with water, they inherently create double-layered structures, called *bilayers*, which shield their hydrophobic regions from the water molecules.

Steroids are lipids that consist of four fused carbon rings. They can mix in between the phospholipid bilayer cell membrane and help maintain its structure, as well as aid in cell signaling.

Enzymes

Enzymes are biological molecules that accelerate the rate of chemical reactions by lowering the activation energy needed to make the reaction proceed. Although most enzymes can be classified as proteins, some are ribonucleic acid (RNA) molecules. Enzymes function by interacting with a specific substrate in order to create a different molecule, or product. Most reactions in cells need enzymes to make them occur at rates fast enough to sustain life.

Basic Genetics

Structure and Function of DNA and RNA

DNA and RNA are made up of *nucleotides*, which are formed from a five-carbon sugar, a nitrogenous base, and one or more phosphate group. While DNA is made up of the sugar deoxyribose, RNA is made up of the sugar ribose. Deoxyribose has one fewer oxygen atom than ribose. DNA and RNA each comprise four nitrogenous bases, three of which they have in common: adenine, guanine, and cytosine. Thymine is found only in DNA and uracil is found only in RNA. Each base has a specific pairing formed by hydrogen bonds, and is known as a *base pair*. Adenine interacts with thymine or uracil, and guanine interacts only with cytosine. While RNA is found in a single strand, DNA is a double-stranded molecule that coils up to form a *double helix* structure.

The specific pairing of the nitrogenous bases allows for the hereditary information stored in DNA to be passed down accurately from parent cells to daughter cells. When chromosomes are *replicated* during cell division, the double-helix DNA is first uncoiled, each strand is replicated, and then two new identical DNA molecules are generated. DNA can also be used as a template for generating proteins. A *single-stranded* RNA is generated from the DNA during a process called *transcription*; proteins are then generated from this RNA in a process called *translation*.

Chromosomes, Genes, Alleles

Chromosomes are found inside the nucleus of cells and contain the hereditary information of the cell in the form of *genes*. Each gene has a specific sequence of DNA that eventually encodes proteins and results in inherited traits. *Alleles* are variations of a specific gene that occur at the same location on the chromosome. For example, blue and brown are two different alleles of the gene that encodes for eye color.

Dominant and Recessive Traits

In genetics, *dominant alleles* are mostly noted in capital letters (A) and *recessive alleles* are mostly noted in lower case letters (a). There are three possible combinations of alleles among dominant and recessive alleles: AA, Aa (known as a heterozygote), and aa. Dominant traits are phenotypes that appear when at least one dominant allele is present in the gene. Dominant alleles are considered to have stronger phenotypes and, when mixed with recessive alleles, will mask the recessive trait. The recessive trait would only appear as the phenotype when the allele combination is "aa" because a dominant allele is not present to mask it.

Mendelian Inheritance

A monk named Gregor Mendel is referred to as the father of genetics. He was responsible for coming up with one of the first models of inheritance in the 1860s. His model included two laws to determine which traits are inherited. These laws still apply today, even after genetics has been studied much more in depth.

- *The Law of Segregation*: Each characteristic has two versions that can be inherited. When two parent cells form daughter cells, the two alleles of the gene segregate and each daughter cell can inherit only one of the alleles from each parent.

- *The Law of Independent Assortment*: The alleles for different traits are inherited independent of one another. In other words, the biological selection of one allele by a daughter cell is not linked to the biological selection of an allele for a different trait by the same daughter cell. The genotype that is inherited is the alleles that are encoded on the gene, and the phenotype is the outward appearance of the physical trait for that gene. For example, "A" is the dominant allele for brown eyes and "a" is the recessive allele for blue eyes; the phenotype of brown eyes would occur for two different genotypes: both "AA" and "Aa."

<u>Punnett Squares</u>
For simple genetic combinations, a *Punnett square* can be used to assess the phenotypic ratios of subsequent generations. In a 2 x 2 cell square, one parent's alleles are set up in columns and the other parent's alleles are set up in rows. The resulting allele combinations are shown in the four internal cells.

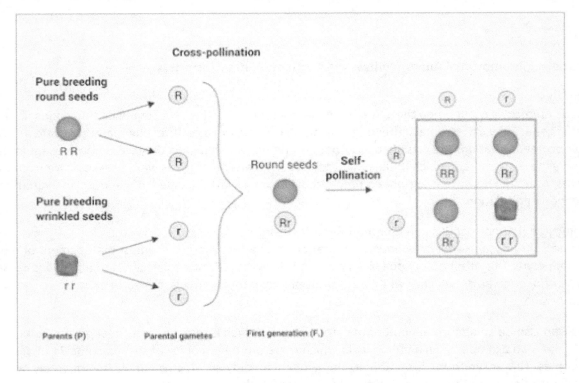

<u>Pedigree</u>
For existing populations where genetic crosses cannot be controlled, phenotype information can be collected over several generations and a *pedigree analysis* can be done to investigate the dominant and

recessive characteristics of specific traits. There are several rules to follow when determining the pedigree of a trait. For dominant alleles:

- Affected individuals have at least one affected parent;
- The phenotype appears in every generation; and
- If both parents are unaffected, their offspring will always be unaffected.

For recessive alleles:

- Unaffected parents can have affected offspring; and
- Affected offspring are male and female.

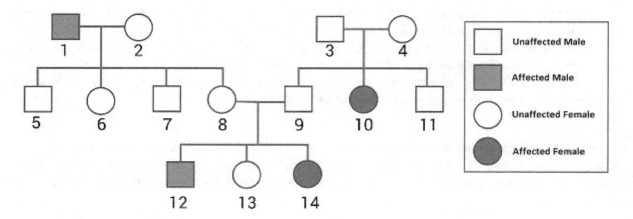

Mutations, Chromosomal Abnormalities, and Common Genetic Disorders

Mutations

Genetic *mutations* occur when there is a permanent alteration in the DNA sequence that codes for a specific gene. They can be small, affecting only one base pair, or large, affecting many genes on a chromosome. Mutations are classified as either hereditary, which means they were also present in the parent gene, or acquired, which means that they occurred after the genes were passed down from the parents. Although mutations are not common, they are an important aspect of genetics and variation in the general population.

Chromosomal Abnormalities and Common Genetic Disorders

Structural chromosomal abnormalities are mutations that affect a large chromosomal segment of more than one gene. This often occurs due to an error in cell division. Acute myelogenous leukemia is caused by a *translocation error*, which is when a segment of one chromosome is moved to another chromosome.

There can also be an abnormal number of chromosomes, which is referred to as *aneuploidy*. Down syndrome is an example of an aneuploidy in which there are three copies of chromosome 21 instead of two copies. Turner syndrome is another example of aneuploidy, in which a female is completely or partially missing an X chromosome. Without the second X chromosome, these females do not develop all of the typical female physical characteristics and are unable to bear children.

Theory and Key Mechanisms of Evolution

Mechanisms of Evolution

Evolution is the concept that there is one common ancestor for all living organisms, and, over time, genetic variation and mutations cause the development of different species. Charles Darwin came up with a scientific model of evolution based on the idea that individuals within a population can have longer lives (better survival) and higher reproduction rates based on certain specific traits that they have inherited, called *natural selection*. The variation of a trait that enhances survival and reproduction in the environment is the one that gets passed on. The survival and inheritance of these traits through many subsequent generations causes a change in the overall population. The traits that are more advantageous for survival and reproduction become more common in subsequent generations and increase the diversity of the population. For example, when there was a drought in the Galapagos Islands, the finches with large beaks became more populous because they were able to survive on the larger, rougher seeds that were remaining.

Speciation and Isolation Methods

Speciation is the method by which one species splits into two or more species due to either geographic separation, called allopatric speciation, or a reduction in gene flow between varying members of the population, called sympatric speciation. In *allopatric speciation*, one population is divided into two subpopulations. For example, if a drought occurs and a large lake becomes divided into two smaller lakes, each lake is left with its own population that cannot intermingle with the population of the other lake. When the genes of these two subpopulations are no longer mixing with each other, new mutations can arise and natural selection can take place.

In *sympatric speciation*, gene flow in the population is reduced by polyploidy, sexual selection, and habitat differentiation. *Polyploidy* is more common in plants than animals and results when cell division during reproduction creates an extra set of chromosomes. In *sexual selection*, organisms of one sex choose their mate of the opposite sex based on certain traits. If there is high selection for two extreme variations of a trait, sympatric speciation may occur. *Habitat differentiation* occurs when a subpopulation exploits a resource that is not used by the parent population. Both allopatric and sympatric speciation can occur quickly or slowly, and may involve just a few gene changes or many gene changes between the new species.

One important distinguishing factor in the formation of two species is their *reproductive isolation*. Species are characterized by their members' ability to breed and produce viable offspring. When speciation occurs and new species are formed, there must have been a biological barrier that prevented the two species from producing viable offspring.

Following speciation, there are two types of *reproductive barriers* that keep the two populations from mating with each other. These are classified as either prezygotic barriers or postzygotic barriers. *Prezygotic barriers* prevent fertilization via habitat isolation, temporal isolation, and behavioral isolation. Through habitat isolation, two species may inhabit the same area but don't often encounter each other. *Temporal isolation* is when species breed at different times of the day, during different seasons, or during different years, so their mating patterns never coincide. *Behavioral isolation* refers to mating rituals that prevent an organism from recognizing a different species as potential mate.

Other prezygotic barriers block fertilization after a mating attempt. *Mechanical isolation* occurs when anatomical differences prevent fertilization. *Gametic isolation* occurs when the gametes of two species are incompatible.

Supporting Evidence

The Fossil Record

Fossils are the preserved remains of animals and organisms from the distant past. They provide evidence of evolution and can elucidate the homology of both living and extinct species. Looking at the *fossil record* over time can help identify how quickly or slowly evolutionary changes occurred, and can also help match those changes to environmental changes that were occurring concurrently.

Comparative Genetics

In *comparative genetics*, different organisms are compared at a genetic level to look for similarities and differences. DNA sequence, genes, gene order, and other structural features are among the features that may be analyzed in order to look for evolutionary relationships and common ancestors between the organisms. Comparative genetics was useful in elucidating the similarities between humans and chimpanzees and linking their evolutionary history.

Homology

Organisms that developed from a common ancestor often have similar characteristics that function differently. This similarity is known as *homology*. For example, humans, cats, whales, and bats all have bones arranged in the same manner from their shoulders to their digits. However, the bones form arms in humans, forelegs in cats, flippers in whales, and wings in bats, and these forelimbs are used for lifting, walking, swimming, and flying, respectively. The similarity of the bone structure shows a common ancestry, but the functional differences are the product of evolution.

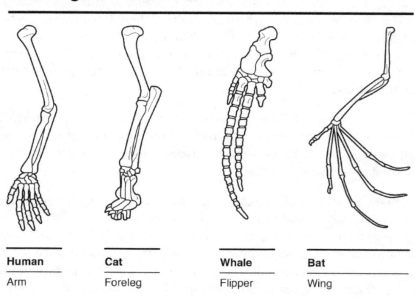

Homologous Structures

Human	**Cat**	**Whale**	**Bat**
Arm	Foreleg	Flipper	Wing

Hierarchical Classification Schemes

Classification Schemes

Taxonomy is the science behind the biological names of organisms. Biologists often refer to organisms by their Latin scientific names to avoid confusion with common names, such as with fish. Jellyfish, crayfish, and silverfish all have the word "fish" in their name, but belong to three different species. In the eighteenth century, Carl Linnaeus invented a naming system for species that included using the Latin scientific name of a species, called the *binomial*, which has two parts: the *genus*, which comes first, and the *specific epithet*, which comes second. Similar species are grouped into the same genus. The Linnean system is the commonly used taxonomic system today and, moving from comprehensive similarities to more general similarities, classifies organisms into their species, genus, family, order, class, phylum, and kingdom. *Homo sapiens* is the Latin scientific name for humans.

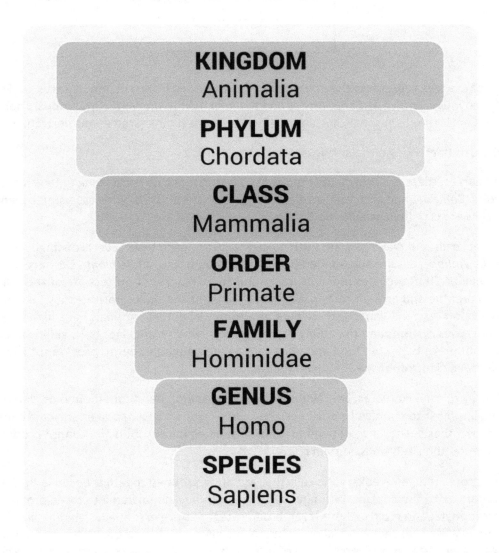

Phylogenetic trees are branching diagrams that represent the evolutionary history of a species. The branch points most often match the classification groups set forth by the Linnean system. Using this system helps elucidate the relationship between different groups of organisms. The diagram below is that of an empty phylogenetic tree:

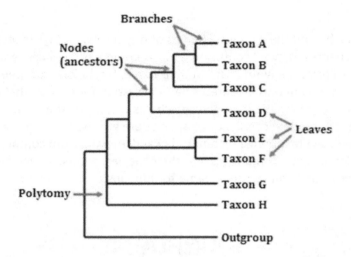

Each branch of the tree represents the divergence of two species from a common ancestor. For example, the coyote is known as Canis latrans and the gray wolf is known as Canis lupus. Their common ancestor, the Canis lepophagus, which is now extinct, is where their shared genus derived.

Characteristics of Bacteria, Animals, Plants, Fungi, and Protists

As discussed earlier, there are two distinct types of cells that make up most living organisms: prokaryotic and eukaryotic. Bacteria (and archaea) are classified as prokaryotic cells, whereas animal, plant, fungi, and protist cells are classified as eukaryotic cells.

Although animal cells and plant cells are both eukaryotic, they each have several distinguishing characteristics. *Animal cells* are surrounded by a plasma membrane, while *plant cells* have a cell wall made up of cellulose that provides more structure and an extra layer of protection for the cell. Animals use oxygen to breathe and give off carbon dioxide, while plants do the opposite—they take in carbon dioxide and give off oxygen. Plants also use light as a source of energy. Animals have highly developed sensory and nervous systems and the ability to move freely, while plants lack both abilities. Animals, however, cannot make their own food and must rely on their environment to provide sufficient nutrition, whereas plants do make their own food.

Fungal cells are typical eukaryotes, containing both a nucleus and membrane-bound organelles. They have a cell wall, similar to plant cells; however, they use oxygen as a source of energy and cannot perform photosynthesis. They also depend on outside sources for nutrition and cannot produce their own food. Of note, their cell walls contain *chitin*.

Protists are a group of diverse eukaryotic cells that are often grouped together because they do not fit into the categories of animal, plant, or fungal cells. They can be categorized into three broad categories: protozoa, protophyta, and molds. These three broad categories are essentially "animal -like," "plant-like," and "fungus-like," respectively. All of them are unicellular and do not form tissues. Besides this simple similarity, protists are a diverse group of organisms with different characteristics, life cycles, and cellular structures.

Major Structures of Plants and Their Functions

Characteristics of Vascular and Nonvascular Plants

Plants that have an extensive vascular transport system are called *vascular plants*. Those plants without a transport system are called *nonvascular plants*. Approximately ninety-three percent of plants that are currently living and reproducing are vascular plants. The cells that comprise the vascular tissue in vascular plants form tubes that transport water and nutrients through the entire plant. Nonvascular plants include mosses, liverworts, and hornworts. They do not retain any water; instead, they transport water using other specialized tissue. They have structures that look like leaves, but are actually just single sheets of cells without a cuticle or stomata.

Structure and Function of Roots, Leaves, and Stems

Roots are responsible for anchoring plants in the ground. They absorb water and nutrients and transport them up through the plant. *Leaves* are the main location of photosynthesis. They contain *stomata*, which are pores used for gas exchange, on their underside to take in carbon dioxide and release oxygen. *Stems* transport materials through the plant and support the plant's body. They contain *xylem*, which conducts water and dissolved nutrients upward through the plant, and *phloem*, which conducts sugars and metabolic products downward through the leaves.

Asexual and Sexual Reproduction

Plants can generate future generations through both asexual and sexual reproduction. Asexually, plants can go through an artificial reproductive technique called *budding*, in which parts from two or more plants of the same species are joined together with the hope that they will begin to grow as a single plant.

Sexual reproduction of flowers can happen in a couple of ways. *Angiosperms* are flowering plants that have seeds. The flowers have male parts that make pollen and female parts that contain ovules. Wind, insects, and other animals carry the pollen from the male part to the female part in a process called *pollination*. Once the ovules are pollinated, or fertilized, they develop into seeds that then develop into new plants. In many angiosperms, the flowers develop into fruit, such as oranges, or even hard nuts, which protect the seeds inside of them.

Nonvascular plants reproduce by sexual reproduction involving *spores*. Parent plants send out spores that contain a set of chromosomes. The spores develop into sperm or eggs, and fertilization is similar to that in humans. Sperm travel to the egg through water in the environment. An embryo forms and then a new plant grows from the embryo. Generally, this happens in damp places.

Growth

Germination is the process of a plant growing from a seed or spore, such as when a seedling sprouts from a seed or a sporeling grows from a spore. Plants then grow by *elongation*. Plant cell walls are modified by the hormone auxin, which allows for cell elongation. This process is regulated by light and phytohormones, which are plant hormones that regulate growth, so plants are often seen growing toward the sun.

Uptake and Transport of Nutrients and Water

Plant roots are responsible for bringing nutrients and water into the plant from the ground. The nutrients are not used as food for the plant, but rather to maintain the plant's health so that the plant can make its own food during photosynthesis. The xylem and phloem in the stem help with transport of water and other substances throughout the plant.

Responses to Stimuli

Because plants have limited mobility, they often respond to stimuli through changes in their growth behavior. *Tropism* is a response to stimuli that causes the plant to grow toward or away from the stimuli:

- *Phototropism*: A reaction to light that causes plants to grow toward the source of the light

- *Thermotropism*: A response to changes in temperature

- *Hydrotropism*: A response to a change in water concentration

- *Gravitropism*: A response to gravity that causes roots to follow the pull of gravity and grow downward, but also causes plant shoots to act against gravity and grow upward

Basic Anatomy and Physiology of Animals, Including the Human Body

Response to Stimuli and Homeostasis

A *stimulus* is a change in the environment, either internal or external, around an organism that is received by a sensory receptor and causes the organism to react. *Homeostasis* is the stable state of an organism. When an organism reacts to stimuli, it works to counteract the change in order to reach homeostasis again.

Exchange with the Environment

Animals exchange gases and nutrients with the environment through several different organ systems. The *respiratory system* mediates the exchange of gas between the air and the circulating blood, mainly through the act of breathing. It filters, warms, and humidifies the air that gets inhaled and then passes it into the blood stream. The main function of the *excretory system* is to eliminate excess material and fluids in the body. The kidneys and bladder work together to filter organic waste products, excess water, and electrolytes from the blood that are generated by the other physiologic systems, and excrete them from the body. The *digestive system* is a group of organs that work together to transform ingested food and liquid into energy, which can then be used by the body as fuel. Once all of the nutrients are absorbed, the waste products are excreted from the body.

Internal Transport and Exchange

The *circulatory system* is composed of the heart and blood vessels. The *heart* acts as a pump and works to circulate blood throughout the body. Blood circulates throughout the body in a system of vessels that includes arteries, veins, and capillaries. It distributes oxygen, nutrients, and hormones to all of the cells in the body. *Arteries* transport oxygen-rich blood from the heart to the rest of the tissues in the body.

The largest artery is the *aorta*. *Veins* collect oxygen-depleted blood from tissues and organs and return it back to the heart. *Capillaries* are the smallest of the blood vessels and do not function individually. Instead, they work together in a unit—called a *capillary bed*—to transport both oxygen-rich and oxygen-poor blood to other vessels.

Control Systems

The *nervous system* is one of the smallest but most complex organ systems in the human body. It consists of all of the neural tissue and is in charge of controlling and adjusting the activities of all of the other systems of the body. It is divided into the *central nervous system (CNS)* and the *peripheral nervous system (PNS)*. The CNS is where intelligence, memory, learning, and emotions are processed. It is responsible for processing and coordinating sensory data and motor commands. The PNS is responsible for relaying sensory information and motor commands between the CNS and peripheral tissues and systems.

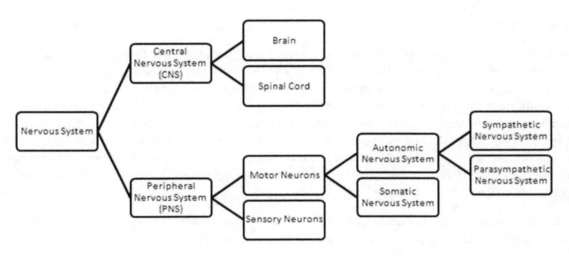

The *endocrine system* is made up of the ductless tissues and glands that secrete hormones into the *interstitial fluids* of the body, which are the fluids that surround tissue cells within the body. This system works closely with the nervous system to regulate the other physiologic systems in order to maintain homeostasis. It acts by releasing hormones into the bloodstream, which are then distributed to the whole body.

Movement and Support

The adult *skeletal system* consists of the 206 bones that make up the skeleton, as well as the cartilage, ligaments, and other connective tissues that stabilize the bones. It provides structural support for the entire body, a framework for the soft tissues and organs to attach to, and acts as a protective barrier for some organs, such as the ribs protecting the heart and lungs, and the vertebrae protecting the spinal cord.

The *muscular system* is responsible for all body movement that occurs. Body movements occur by muscle contractions that cause specific actions or joint movements. There are approximately seven hundred muscles in the body that are attached to the bones of the skeletal system. As mentioned, there are three types of muscle tissue: skeletal, cardiac, and smooth. *Skeletal muscles* are voluntary muscles that attach to bones through tendons. *Cardiac muscle tissue* is found only in the heart and is involuntary. *Smooth muscle tissue* lines the walls of hollow structures, such as blood vessels, the stomach, and the bladder, and is involuntary. When smooth muscle tissue contracts, the structure it lines narrows or constricts.

Reproduction and Development

The *reproductive system* is responsible for producing and maintaining functional reproductive cells in the human body. The human male and female reproductive systems are very different from each other. The male gonads, called *testes*, mainly secrete testosterone, which is a steroid hormone that controls the development and maintenance of male physical characteristics. They also produce *sperm cells*, which are responsible for fertilizing the female reproductive cell in order to produce offspring. The female gonads, called *ovaries*, generally produce one immature egg per month. They are also responsible for secreting the hormones estrogen and progesterone. Once an egg is fertilized by a sperm cell, an *embryo* develops. After approximately 40 weeks of gestation, a baby is born.

Immune System

The *immune system* comprises cells, tissues, and organs that work together to protect the body from harmful foreign invaders. It is important for the body's immune system to be able to distinguish between *pathogens*, such as viruses and parasites, and the body's own healthy tissue. There are two types of immune systems that work to defend the body against infection: the innate system and the adaptive system. The *innate immune system* works without having a memory of the pathogens it defended against previously. The *adaptive immune system* creates a memory of the pathogen that it fought against, so that the body can respond again in an efficient manner the next time the pathogen is encountered. When *antigens* or *allergens* such as pollen are encountered, antibodies are secreted to inactivate the antigen and protect the body.

If the immune system is not functioning properly, the body may develop an *autoimmune disorder*. In this case, the body cannot distinguish between itself and foreign pathogens, so it attacks itself unnecessarily.

Key Aspects of Ecology

Population Dynamics

Population dynamics is the study of the composition of populations, including size, age, and the biological and environmental processes that cause changes. These can include immigration, emigration, births, and deaths.

Growth Curves and Carrying Capacity

Population dynamics can be characterized by *growth curves*. Growth can either be *unrestricted*, which is modeled by an exponential curve, or *restricted*, which is modeled by a logistic curve. Population growth can be restricted by environmental factors such as the availability of food and water sources, habitat, and other necessities. The *carrying capacity* of a population is the maximum population size that an environment can sustain indefinitely, given all of the above factors.

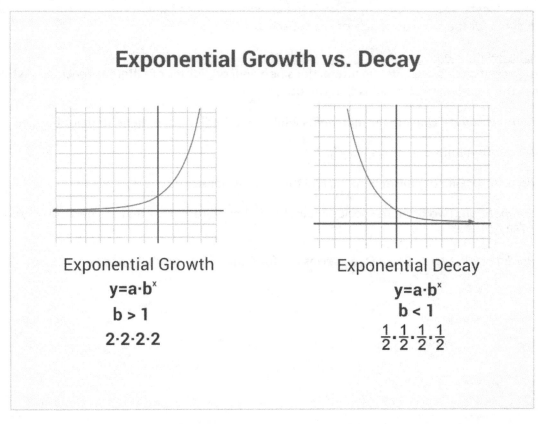

Behavior

Different species within a population can act differently regarding their environment. Some species display *territoriality*, which is a specific type of competition that excludes other species from a given area. It can be shown through specific animal calls, intimidating behavior, or marking an area with scents, and is often a display of defense.

Intraspecific Relationships

Intraspecific relationships is a term that describes the competition and cooperation between organisms that belong to the same species. They may compete for the same food sources, or for mates that are necessary for their personal survival and reproduction. Stronger organisms may display dominance that allows them to reside at the top of a social hierarchy and obtain better food and higher quality mates. However, organisms may also cooperate with each other in order to benefit the larger group; for instance, they may divide laborious activities among themselves.

Community Ecology

An *ecological community* is a group of species that interact and live in the same location. Because of their shared environment, they tend to have a large influence on each other.

Niche
An *ecological niche* is the role that a species plays in its environment, including how it finds its food and shelter. It could be a predator of a different species, or prey for a larger species.

Species Diversity
Species diversity is the number of different species that cohabitate in an ecological community. It has two different facets: *species richness*, which is the general number of species, and *species evenness*, which accounts for the population size of each species.

Interspecific Relationships
Interspecific relationships include the interactions between organisms of different species. The following list defines the common relationships that can occur:

- *Commensalism*: One organism benefits while the other is neither benefited nor harmed

- *Mutualism*: Both organisms benefit

- *Parasitism*: One organism benefits and the other is harmed

- *Competition*: Two or more species compete for limited resources that are necessary for their survival

- *Predation (Predator-Prey)*: One species is a food source for another species

Ecosystems

An *ecosystem* includes all of the living organisms and nonliving components of an environment (each community) and their interactions with each other.

Biomes
A *biome* is a group of plants and animals that are found in many different continents and have the same characteristics because of the similar climates in which they live. Each biome is composed of all of the ecosystems in that area. Five primary types of biomes are aquatic, deserts, forests, grasslands, and tundra. The sum total of all biomes comprises the Earth's biosphere.

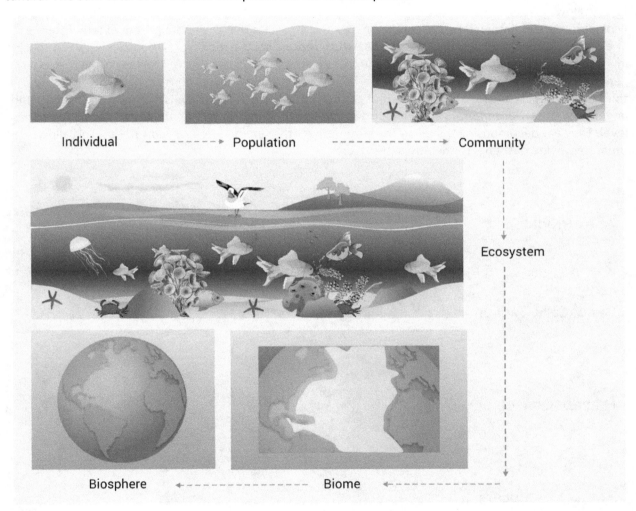

Stability and Disturbances
Ecological stability is the ability of an ecosystem to withstand changes that are occurring within it. With *regenerative stability*, an ecosystem may change, but then quickly return to its previous state. *Constant stability* occurs in ecosystems that remain unchanged despite the changes going on around them.

An *ecological disturbance* is a change in the environment that causes a larger change in the ecosystem. Smaller disturbances include fires and floods. Larger disturbances include the *climate change* that is currently occurring. Gas emissions from human activity are causing the atmosphere to warm up, which is changing the Earth's water systems and making weather more extreme. The increase in temperature is causing greater evaporation of the water sources on Earth, creating droughts and depleting natural water sources. This has also caused many of the Earth's glaciers to begin melting, which can change the salinity of the oceans.

Changes in the environment can cause an *ecological succession* to occur, which is the change in structure of the species that coexist in an ecological community. When the environment changes, resources available to the different species also change. For example, the formation of sand dunes or a forest fire would change the environment enough to allow a change in the social hierarchy of the coexisting species.

<u>Energy Flow</u>
Ecosystems are maintained by cycling the energy and nutrients that they obtain from external sources. The process can be diagramed in a *food web*, which represents the feeding relationship between species in a community. The different levels of the food web are called *trophic levels*. The first trophic level generally consists of plants, algae, and bacteria. The second trophic level consists of herbivores. The third trophic level consists of predators that eat herbivores. The trophic levels continue on to larger and larger predators. *Decomposers* are an important part of the food chain that are not at a specific trophic level. They eat decomposing things on the ground that other animals do not want to eat. This allows them to provide nutrients to their own predators.

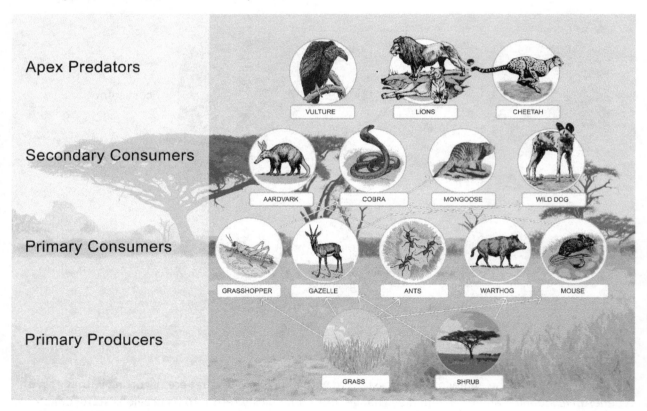

<u>Biogeochemical Cycles</u>
Biogeochemical cycles are the pathways by which chemicals move through the *biotic*, or biospheric, and *abiotic*, or atmospheric, parts of the Earth. The most important biogeochemical cycles include the water, carbon, and nitrogen cycles. *Water* goes through an evaporation, condensation, and precipitation cycle. *Nitrogen* makes up seventy-eight percent of the Earth's atmosphere and can affect the rate of many

ecosystem processes, such as production of the primary producers at the first trophic level of the food web. The *carbon cycle* has many steps that are vitally important for sustaining life on Earth.

The water cycle:

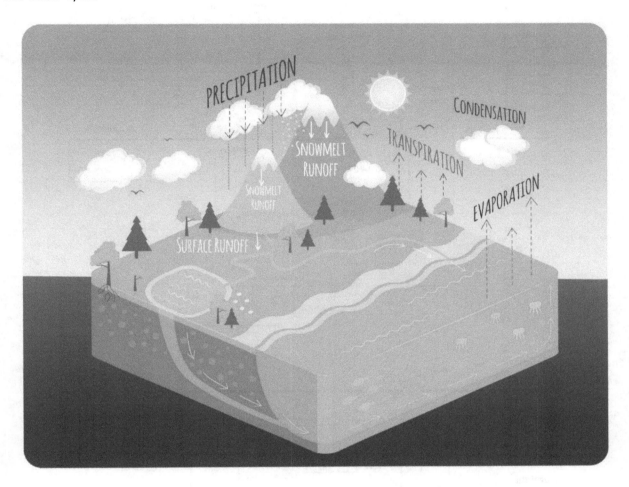

The nitrogen cycle:

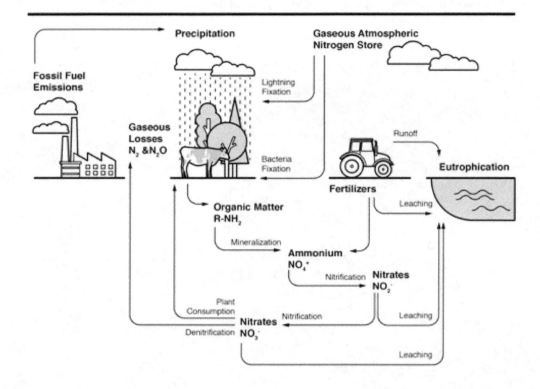

The carbon cycle:

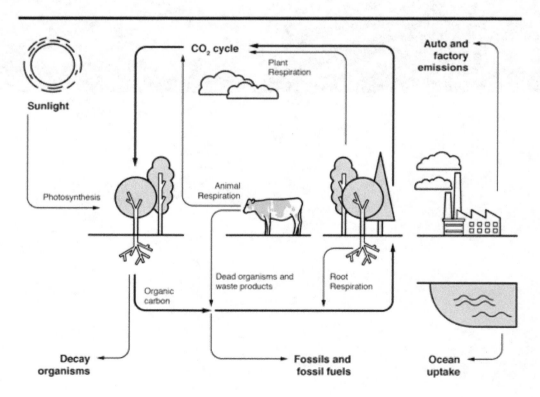

Practice Questions

1. What types of molecules can move through a cell membrane by passive transport?
   a. Complex sugars
   b. Non-lipid soluble molecules
   c. Oxygen
   d. Molecules moving from areas of low concentration to areas of high concentration

2. What is ONE feature that both prokaryotes and eukaryotes have in common?
   a. A plasma membrane
   b. A nucleus enclosed by a membrane
   c. Organelles
   d. A nucleoid

3. What is the LAST phase of mitosis?
   a. Prophase
   b. Telophase
   c. Anaphase
   d. Metaphase

4. How many daughter cells are formed from one parent cell during meiosis?
   a. One
   b. Two
   c. Three
   d. Four

5. In which organelle do eukaryotes carry out aerobic respiration?
   a. Golgi apparatus
   b. Nucleus
   c. Mitochondrion
   d. Cytosol

6. What kind of energy do plants use in photosynthesis to create chemical energy?
   a. Light
   b. Electric
   c. Nuclear
   d. Cellular

7. What type of biological molecule is a monosaccharide?
   a. Protein
   b. Carbohydrate
   c. Nucleic acid
   d. Lipid

8. Which level of protein structure is defined by the folds and coils of the protein's polypeptide backbone?
    a. Primary
    b. Secondary
    c. Tertiary
    d. Quaternary

9. Which base pairs with adenine in RNA?
    a. Thymine
    b. Guanine
    c. Cytosine
    d. Uracil

10. With which genotype would the recessive phenotype appear, if the dominant allele is marked with "A" and the recessive allele is marked with "a"?
    a. AA
    b. aa
    c. Aa
    d. aA

11. What is ONE reason why speciation can occur?
    a. Geographic separation
    b. Seasons
    c. Daylight
    d. A virus

12. What is the broadest, or LEAST specialized, classification of the Linnean taxonomic system?
    a. Species
    b. Family
    c. Domain
    d. Phylum

13. How are fungi similar to plants?
    a. They have a cell wall
    b. They contain chloroplasts
    c. They perform photosynthesis
    d. They use carbon dioxide as a source of energy

14. What important function are the roots of plants responsible for?
    a. Absorbing water from the surrounding environment
    b. Performing photosynthesis
    c. Conducting sugars downward through the leaves
    d. Supporting the plant body

15. Which of the following would occur in response to a change in water concentration?
    a. Phototropism
    b. Thermotropism
    c. Gravitropism
    d. Hydrotropism

16. What is the MAIN function of the respiratory system?
    a. To eliminate waste through the kidneys and bladder
    b. To exchange gas between the air and circulating blood
    c. To transform food and liquids into energy
    d. To excrete waste from the body

17. What type of vessel carries oxygen-rich blood from the heart to other tissues of the body?
    a. Veins
    b. Intestines
    c. Bronchioles
    d. Arteries

18. Which system comprises the 206 bones of the body?
    a. Skeletal
    b. Muscular
    c. Endocrine
    d. Reproductive

19. Which factor is NOT a consideration in population dynamics?
    a. Size and age of population
    b. Immigration
    c. Hair color
    d. Number of births

20. Which type of diagram describes the cycling of energy and nutrients of an ecosystem?
    a. Food web
    b. Phylogenetic tree
    c. Fossil record
    d. Pedigree chart

Answers and Explanations

1. C: Molecules that are soluble in lipids, like fats, sterols, and vitamins (A, D, E and K), for example, are able to move in and out of a cell using passive transport. Water and oxygen are also able to move in and out of the cell without the use of cellular energy. Complex sugars and non-lipid soluble molecules are too large to move through the cell membrane without relying on active transport mechanisms. Molecules naturally move from areas of high concentration to those of lower concentration. It requires active transport to move molecules in the opposite direction, as suggested by Choice *D*.

2. A: Both types of cells are enclosed by plasma membranes with cytosol on the inside. Prokaryotes contain a nucleoid and do not have organelles; eukaryotes contain a nucleus enclosed by a membrane, as well as organelles.

3. B: During telophase, two nuclei form at each end of the cell and nuclear envelopes begin to form around each nucleus. The nucleoli reappear, and the chromosomes become less compact. The microtubules are broken down by the cell, and mitosis is complete. The process begins with prophase as the mitotic spindles begin to form from centrosomes. Prometaphase follows, with the breakdown of the nuclear envelope and the further condensing of the chromosomes. Next, metaphase occurs when the microtubules are stretched across the cell and the chromosomes align at the metaphase plate. Finally, in the last step before telophase, anaphase occurs as the sister chromatids break apart and form chromosomes.

4. D: Meiosis has the same phases as mitosis, except that they occur twice—once in meiosis I and once in meiosis II. During meiosis I, the cell splits into two. Each cell contains two sets of chromosomes. Next, during meiosis II, the two intermediate daughter cells divide again, producing four total haploid cells that each contain one set of chromosomes.

5. C: The mitochondrion is often called the powerhouse of the cell and is one of the most important structures for maintaining regular cell function. It is where aerobic cellular respiration occurs and where most of the cell's ATP is generated. The number of mitochondria in a cell varies greatly from organism to organism and from cell to cell. Cells that require more energy, like muscle cells, have more mitochondria.

6. A: Photosynthesis is the process of converting light energy into chemical energy, which is then stored in sugar and other organic molecules. The photosynthetic process takes place in the thylakoids inside chloroplast in plants. Chlorophyll is a green pigment that lives in the thylakoid membranes and absorbs photons from light.

7. B: Carbohydrates consist of sugars. The simplest sugar molecule is called a monosaccharide and has the molecular formula of CH_2O, or a multiple of that formula. Monosaccharides are important molecules for cellular respiration. Their carbon skeleton can also be used to rebuild new small molecules. Lipids are fats, proteins are formed via amino acids, and nucleic acid is found in DNA and RNA.

8. B: The secondary structure of a protein refers to the folds and coils that are formed by hydrogen bonding between the slightly charged atoms of the polypeptide backbone. The primary structure is the sequence of amino acids, similar to the letters in a long word. The tertiary structure is the overall shape of the molecule that results from the interactions between the side chains that are linked to the polypeptide backbone. The quaternary structure is the complete protein structure that occurs when a protein is made up of two or more polypeptide chains.

9. D: DNA and RNA each contain four nitrogenous bases, three of which they have in common: adenine, guanine, and cytosine. Thymine is only found in DNA, and uracil is only found in RNA. Adenine interacts with uracil in RNA, and with thymine in DNA. Guanine always pairs with cytosine in both DNA and RNA.

10. B: Dominant alleles are considered to have stronger phenotypes and, when mixed with recessive alleles, will mask the recessive trait. The recessive trait would only appear as the phenotype when the allele combination is "aa" because a dominant allele is not present to mask it.

11. A: Speciation is the method by which one species splits into two or more species. In allopatric speciation, one population is divided into two subpopulations. If a drought occurs and a large lake becomes divided into two smaller lakes, each lake is left with its own population that cannot intermingle with the population of the other lake. When the genes of these two subpopulations are no longer mixing with each other, new mutations can arise and natural selection can take place.

12. C: In the Linnean system, organisms are classified as follows, moving from comprehensive and specific similarities to fewer and more general similarities: species, genus, family, order, class, phylum, kingdom, and domain. A popular mnemonic device to remember the Linnean system is "Dear King Philip came over for good soup."

13. A: Fungal cells have a cell wall, similar to plant cells; however, they use oxygen as a source of energy and cannot perform photosynthesis. Because they do not perform photosynthesis, fungal cells do not contain chloroplasts.

14. A: Roots are responsible for absorbing water and nutrients that will get transported up through the plant. They also anchor the plant to the ground. Photosynthesis occurs in leaves, stems transport materials through the plant and support the plant body, and phloem moves sugars downward to the leaves.

15. D: Tropism is a response to stimuli that causes the plant to grow toward or away from the stimuli. Hydrotropism is a response to a change in water concentration. Phototropism is a reaction to light that causes plants to grow toward the source of the light. Thermotropism is a response to changes in temperature. Gravitropism is a response to gravity that causes roots to follow the pull of gravity and grow downward, but also causes plant shoots to act against gravity and grow upward.

16. B: The respiratory system mediates the exchange of gas between the air and the circulating blood, mainly by the act of breathing. It filters, warms, and humidifies the air that gets breathed in and then passes it into the blood stream. The digestive system transforms food and liquids into energy and helps excrete waste from the body. Eliminating waste via the kidneys and bladder is a function of the urinary system.

17. D: Arteries carry oxygen-rich blood from the heart to the other tissues of the body. Veins carry oxygen-poor blood back to the heart. Intestines carry digested food through the body. Bronchioles are passageways that carry air from the nose and mouth to the lungs.

18. A: The skeletal system consists of the 206 bones that make up the skeleton, as well as the cartilage, ligaments, and other connective tissues that stabilize the bones. The skeletal system provides structural support for the entire body, a framework for the soft tissues and organs to attach to, and acts as a protective barrier for some organs, such as the ribs protecting the heart and lungs, and the vertebrae protecting the spinal cord. The muscular system includes skeletal muscles, cardiac muscle, and the smooth muscles found on the inside of blood vessels. The endocrine system uses ductless glands to produce hormones that help maintain hemostasis, and the reproductive system is responsible for the productions of egg and sperm cells.

19. C: Population dynamics looks at the composition of populations, including size and age, and the biological and environmental processes that cause changes. These can include immigration, emigration, births, and deaths.

20. A: Ecosystems are maintained by cycling the energy and nutrients that they obtain from external sources. The process can be diagramed in a food web, which represents the feeding relationship between the species in a community. A phylogenetic tree shows inferred evolutionary relationships among species and is similar to the fossil record. A pedigree chart shows occurrences of phenotypes of a particular gene through the generations of an organism.

Earth and Space Science

Physical Geology

Types and Basic Characteristics of Rocks and Minerals and Their Formation Processes

The Rock Cycle

Although it may not always be apparent, rocks are constantly being destroyed while new ones are created in a process called the *rock cycle*. This cycle is driven by plate tectonics and the water cycle, which are discussed in detail later. The rock cycle starts with *magma*, the molten rock found deep within the Earth. As magma moves toward the Earth's surface, it hardens and transforms into igneous rock. Then, over time, igneous rock is broken down into tiny pieces called *sediment* that are eventually deposited all over the surface. As more and more sediment accumulates, the weight of the newer sediment compresses the older sediment underneath and creates sedimentary rock. As sedimentary rock is pushed deeper below the surface, the high pressure and temperature transform it into metamorphic rock. This metamorphic rock can either rise to the surface again or sink even deeper and melt back into magma, thus starting the cycle again.

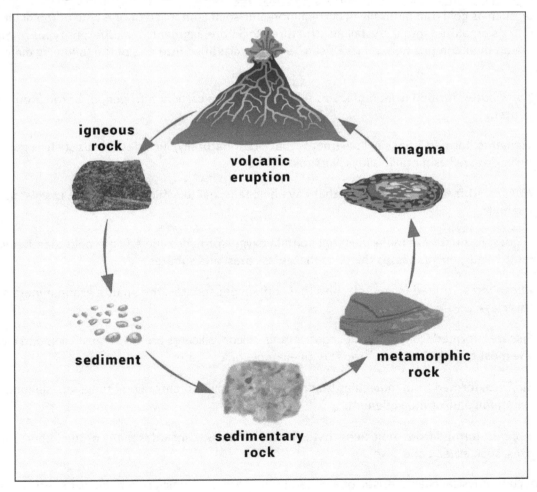

Characteristics of Rocks and Their Formation Processes

There are three main types of rocks: sedimentary, igneous, and metamorphic. Aside from physical characteristics, one of their main differences is how they are created. *Sedimentary rocks* are formed at the surface, on land and in bodies of water, through processes called deposition and cementation. They can be classified as clastic, biochemical, and chemical. *Clastic rocks*, such as sandstone, are composed of other pieces of inorganic rocks and sediment. *Biochemical rocks* are created from an organic material, such as coal, forming from dead plant life. *Chemical rocks* are created from the deposition of dissolved minerals, such as calcium salts that form stalagmites and stalactites in caves.

Igneous rocks are created when magma solidifies at or near the Earth's surface. When they're formed at the surface, (i.e. from volcanic eruption), they are *extrusive*. When they form below the surface, they're called *intrusive*. Examples of extrusive rocks are obsidian and tuff, while rocks like granite are intrusive.

Metamorphic rocks are the result of a transformation from other rocks. Based on appearance, these rocks are classified as foliated or non-foliated. *Foliated rocks* are created from compression in one direction, making them appear layered or folded like slate. *Non-foliated rocks* are compressed from all directions, giving them a more homogenous appearance, such as marble.

Characteristics of Minerals and Their Formation Processes

A *mineral*, such as gold, is a naturally occurring inorganic solid composed of one type of molecule or element that's organized into a crystalline structure. Rocks are aggregates of different types of minerals. Depending on their composition, minerals can be mainly classified into one of the following eight groups:

- *Carbonates*: formed from molecules that have either a carbon, nitrogen, or boron atom at the center.

- *Elements*: formed from single elements that occur naturally; includes metals such as gold and nickel, as well as metallic alloys like brass.

- *Halides:* formed from molecules that have halogens; halite, which is table salt, is a classic example.

- *Oxides*: formed from molecules that contain oxygen or hydroxide and are held together with ionic bonds; encompasses the phosphates, silicates, and sulfates.

- *Phosphates*: formed from molecules that contain phosphates; the apatite group minerals are in this class.

- *Silicates*: formed from molecules that contain silicon, silicates are the largest class and usually the most complex minerals; topaz is an example of a silicate.

- *Sulfates*: formed from molecules that contain either sulfur, chromium, tungsten, selenium, tellurium, and/or molybdenum.

- *Sulfides*: formed from molecules that contain sulfide (S^{2-}); includes many of the important metal ores, such as lead and silver.

One important physical characteristic of a mineral is its *hardness*, which is defined as its resistance to scratching. When two crystals are struck together, the harder crystal will scratch the softer crystal. The most common measure of hardness is the Mohs Hardness Scale, which ranges from 1 to 10, with 10 being the hardest. Diamonds are rated 10 on the Mohs Hardness Scale, and talc, which was once used to make baby powder, is rated 1. Other important characteristics of minerals include *luster* or shine, *color,* and *cleavage*, which is the natural plane of weakness at which a specific crystal breaks.

Erosion, Weathering, and Deposition of Earth's Surface Materials and Soil Formation

Erosion and Deposition
Erosion is the process of moving rock and occurs when rock and sediment are picked up and transported. Wind, water, and ice are the primary factors for erosion. *Deposition* occurs when the particles stop moving and settle onto a surface, which can happen through gravity or involve processes such as precipitation or flocculation. *Precipitation* is the solidification or crystallization of dissolved ions that occurs when a solution is oversaturated. *Flocculation* is similar to coagulation and occurs when colloid materials (materials that aren't dissolved but are suspended in the medium) aggregate or clump until they are too heavy to remain suspended.

Chemical and Physical (Mechanical) Weathering
Weathering is the process of breaking down rocks through mechanical or chemical changes. Mechanical forces include animal contact, wind, extreme weather, and the water cycle. These physical forces don't alter the composition of rocks. In contrast, chemical weathering transforms rock composition. When water and minerals interact, they can start chemical reactions and form new or secondary minerals from the original rock. In chemical weathering, the processes of oxidation and hydrolysis are important. When rain falls, it dissolves atmospheric carbon dioxide and becomes acidic. With sulfur dioxide and nitrogen oxide in the atmosphere from volcanic eruptions or burning fossil fuels, the rainfall becomes even more acidic and creates acid rain. Acidic rain can dissolve the rock that it falls upon.

Characteristics of Soil
Soil is a combination of minerals, organic materials, liquids, and gases. There are three main types of soil, as defined by their compositions, going from coarse to fine: sand, silt, and clay. Large particles, such as those found in sand, affect how water moves through the soil, while tiny clay particles can be chemically active and bind with water and nutrients. An important characteristic of soil is its ability to form a crust when dehydrated. In general, the finer the soil, the harder the crust, which is why clay (and not sand) is used to make pottery.

There are many different classes of soil, but the components are always sand, silt, or clay. Below is a chart used by the United States Department of Agriculture (USDA) to define soil types:

The United States Department of Agriculture's (USDA's) Soil Types

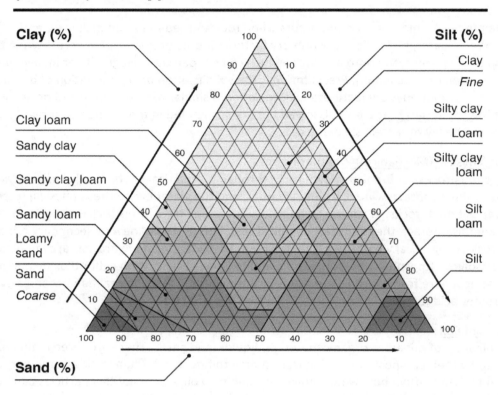

Loam is a term for soil that is a mixture of sand, silt, and clay. It's also the soil most commonly used for agriculture and gardening.

Porosity and Permeability

Porosity and permeability refer to how water moves through rock and soil underground. *Porosity* is a measure of the open space in a rock. This space can be between grains or within cracks and cavities in the rock. *Permeability* is a measure of the ease with which water can move through a porous rock. Therefore, rock that's more porous is also more permeable. When a rock is more permeable, it's less effective as a water purifier because dirty particles in the water can pass through porous rock.

Runoff and Infiltration

An important function of soil is to absorb water to be used by plants or released into groundwater. *Infiltration capacity* is the maximum amount of water that can enter soil at any given time and is regulated by the soil's porosity and composition. For example, sandy soils have larger pores than clays, allowing water to infiltrate them easier and faster. *Runoff* is water that moves across land's surface and may end up in a stream or a rut in the soil. Runoff generally occurs after the soil's infiltration capacity is reached. However, during heavy rainfalls, water may reach the soil's surface at a faster rate than infiltration can occur, causing runoff without soil saturation. In addition, if the ground is frozen and the soil's pores are blocked by ice, runoff may occur without water infiltrating the soil.

Earth's Basic Structure and Internal Processes

Earth's Layers

Earth has three major layers: a thin solid outer surface or *crust*, a dense *core,* and a *mantle* between them that contains most of the Earth's matter. This layout resembles an egg, where the eggshell is the crust, the mantle is the egg white, and the core is the yolk. The outer crust of the Earth consists of igneous or sedimentary rocks over metamorphic rocks. Together with the upper portion of the mantle, it forms the *lithosphere*, which is broken into tectonic plates.

Major plates of the lithosphere

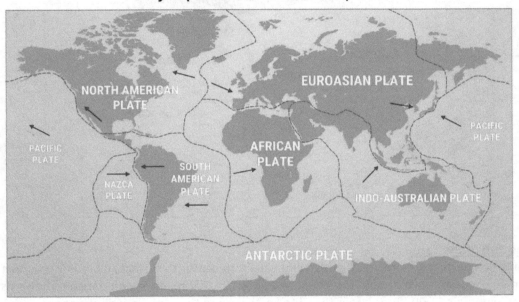

The mantle can be divided into three zones. The *upper mantle* is adjacent to the crust and composed of solid rock. Below the upper mantle is the *transition zone*. The *lower mantle* below the transition zone is a layer of completely solid rock. Underneath the mantle is the molten *outer core* followed by the compact, solid *inner core*. The inner and outer cores contain the densest elements, consisting of mostly iron and nickel.

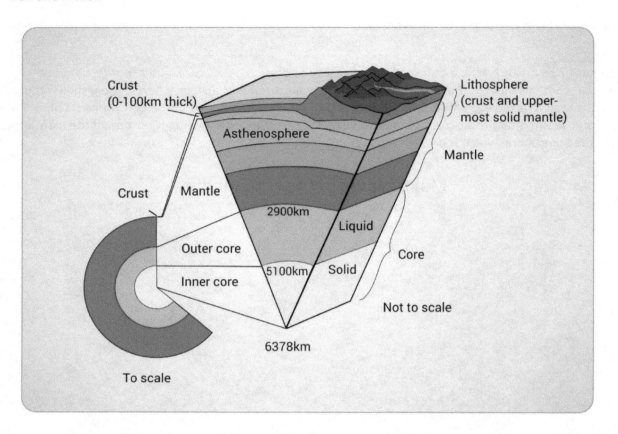

Shape and Size of the Earth

The Earth isn't a perfect sphere; it's slightly elliptical. From center to surface, its radius is almost 4,000 miles, and its circumference around the equator is about 24,902 miles. In comparison, the Sun's radius is 432,288 miles—over 1,000 times larger than the Earth's—and the Moon's radius is about 1,000 miles.

Geographical Features

The Earth's surface is dynamic and consists of various landforms. As tectonic plates are pushed together, *mountains* are formed. *Canyons* are deep trenches that are usually created by plates moving apart, but can also be created by constant weathering and erosion from rivers and runoff. *Deltas* are flat, triangular stretches of land formed by rivers that deposit sediment and water into the ocean. *Sand dunes* are mountains of sand located in desert areas or the bottom of the ocean. They are formed by wind and water movement when there's an absence of plants or other features that would otherwise hold the sand in place.

The Earth's Magnetic Field

The Earth's magnetic field is created by the magnetic forces that extend from the Earth's interior to outer space. It can be modeled as a magnetic dipole tilted about 10 degrees from the Earth's rotational axis, as if a bar magnet was placed at an angle inside the Earth's core. The geomagnetic pole located near Greenland in the northern hemisphere is actually the south pole of the Earth's magnetic field, and vice versa for the southern geomagnetic pole. The *magnetosphere* is the Earth's magnetic field, which extends tens of thousands of kilometers into space and protects the Earth and the atmosphere from damaging solar wind and cosmic rays.

Plate Tectonics Theory and Evidence
The theory of *plate tectonics* hypothesizes that the continents weren't always separated like they are today, but were once joined and slowly drifted apart. Evidence for this theory is based upon evolution and the fossil record. Fossils of one species were found in regions of the world now separated by an ocean. It's unlikely that a single species could have travelled across the ocean or that two separate species evolved into a single species.

Folding and Faulting
The exact number of tectonic plates is debatable, but scientists estimate there are around nine to fifteen major plates and almost 40 minor plates. The line where two plates meet is called a *fault*. The San Andreas Fault is where the Pacific and North American plates meet. Faults or boundaries are classified depending on the interaction between plates. Two plates collide at *convergent boundaries*. *Divergent boundaries* occur when two plates move away from each other. Tectonic plates can move vertically and horizontally.

Continental Drift, Seafloor Spreading, Magnetic Reversals
The movement of tectonic plates is similar to pieces of wood floating in a pool of water. They can bob up and down as well as bump, slide, and move away from each other. These different interactions create the Earth's landscape. The collision of plates can create mountain ranges, while their separation can create canyons or underwater chasms. One plate can also slide atop another and push it down into the Earth's hot mantle, creating magma and volcanoes, in a process called *subduction*.

Unlike a regular magnet, the Earth's magnetic field changes over time because it's generated by the motion of molten iron alloys in the outer core. Although the magnetic poles can wander geographically, they do so at such a slow rate that they don't affect the use of compasses in navigation. However, at irregular intervals that are several hundred thousand years long, the fields can reverse, with the north and south magnetic poles switching places.

Characteristics of Volcanoes
Volcanoes are mountainous structures that act as vents to release pressure and magma from the Earth's crust. During an *eruption*, the pressure and magma are released, and volcanoes smoke, rumble, and throw ash and *lava*, or molten rock, into the air. *Hot spots* are volcanic regions of the mantle that are hotter than surrounding regions.

Characteristics of Earthquakes
Earthquakes occur when tectonic plates slide or collide as a result of the crust suddenly releasing energy. Stress in the Earth's outer layer pushes together two faults. The motion of the planes of the fault continues until something makes them stop. The *epicenter* of an earthquake is the point on the surface directly above where the fault is slipping. If the epicenter is located under a body of water, the earthquake may cause a *tsunami*, a series of large, forceful waves.

Seismic waves and Triangulation
Earthquakes cause *seismic waves*, which travel through the Earth's layers and give out low-frequency acoustic energy. Triangulation of seismic waves helps scientists determine the origin of an earthquake.

The Water Cycle

Evaporation and Condensation
The *water cycle* is the cycling of water between its three physical states: solid, liquid, and gas. The Sun's thermal energy heats surface water so it evaporates. As water vapor collects in the atmosphere from evaporation, it eventually reaches a saturation level where it condenses and forms clouds heavy with water droplets.

Precipitation
When the droplets condense as clouds get heavy, they fall as different forms of precipitation, such as rain, snow, hail, fog, and sleet. *Advection* is the process of evaporated water moving from the ocean and falling over land as precipitation.

Runoff and Infiltration
Runoff and *infiltration* are important parts of the water cycle because they provide water on the surface available for evaporation. Runoff can add water to oceans and aid in the advection process. Infiltration provides water to plants and aids in the transpiration process.

Transpiration
Transpiration is an evaporation-like process that occurs in plants and soil. Water from the stomata of plants and from pores in soil evaporates into water vapor and enters the atmosphere.

Historical Geology

Historical Geology

Principle of Uniformitarianism
Uniformitarianism is the assumption that natural laws and processes haven't changed and apply everywhere in the universe. In geology, uniformitarianism includes the *gradualist model*, which states that "the present is the key to the past" and claims that natural laws functioned at the same rates as observed today.

Basic Principles of Relative Age Dating
Relative age dating is the determination of the relative order of past events without determining absolute age. The Law of Superposition states that older geological layers are deeper than more recent layers. Rocks and fossils can be used to compare one stratigraphic column with another. A *stratigraphic column* is a drawing that describes the vertical location of rocks in a cliff wall or underground. Correlating these columns from different geographic areas allows scientists to understand the relationships between different areas and strata. Before the discovery of radiometric dating, geologists used this technique to determine the ages of different materials. Relative dating can only determine the sequential order of events, not the exact time they occurred. The Law of Fossil Succession states that

when the same kinds of fossils are found in rocks from different locations, the rocks are likely the same age.

Trace fossils   Remain   Layer Analysis

Absolute (Radiometric) Dating

Absolute or *radiometric dating* is the process of determining age on a specified chronology in archaeology and geology. It provides a numerical age by measuring the radioactive decay of elements (such as carbon-14) trapped in rocks or minerals and using the known rate of decay to determine how much time has passed. *Uranium-lead dating* can be used to date some of the oldest rocks on Earth, from 1 million to over 4.5 billion years old.

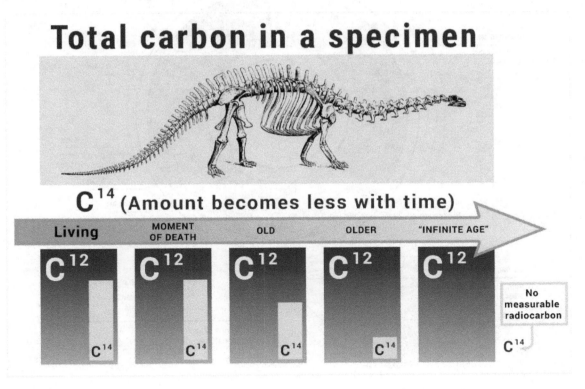

Geologic Time Scale

The *geological time scale* is a system that correlates geological strata to time. It's used by scientists to describe the timing and relationships of past natural events. Radiometric dating calculates that the Earth is around 4.55 billion years old. The geology of the Earth's past is organized into units following events that occurred in each period. The diagram below is geologic time scale represented in a clock-face format. The 12 o'clock position represents the formation of the Earth as well as present time. It shows important events in the Earth's history in relation to each other. In the picture, Ma represents millions of years and Ga represents billions of years.

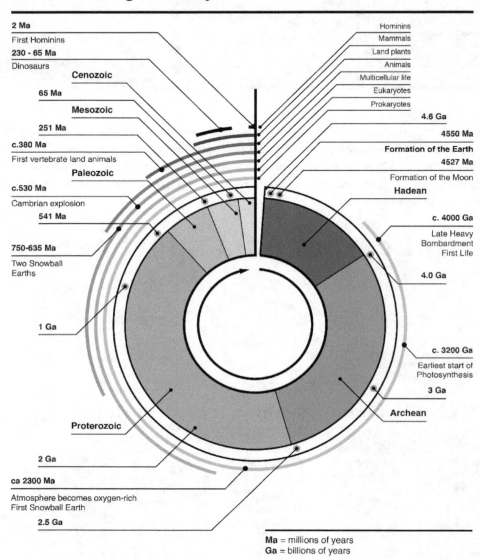

Earth's Geologic History

2 Ma
First Hominins
230 - 65 Ma
Dinosaurs
Cenozoic
65 Ma
Mesozoic
251 Ma
c.380 Ma
First vertebrate land animals
Paleozoic
c.530 Ma
Cambrian explosion
541 Ma
750-635 Ma
Two Snowball Earths
1 Ga
Proterozoic
2 Ga
ca 2300 Ma
Atmosphere becomes oxygen-rich
First Snowball Earth
2.5 Ga

Hominins
Mammals
Land plants
Animals
Multicellular life
Eukaryotes
Prokaryotes
4.6 Ga
4550 Ma
Formation of the Earth
4527 Ma
Formation of the Moon
Hadean
c. 4000 Ga
Late Heavy Bombardment
First Life
4.0 Ga
c. 3200 Ga
Earliest start of Photosynthesis
3 Ga
Archean

Ma = millions of years
Ga = billions of years

148

<u>Fossil Record as Evidence of the Origin and Development of Life</u>
The *fossil record* is the location of fossils throughout the Earth's surface layers. Deeper fossils are older than the fossils above. Scientists use the fossil record to determine when certain organisms existed and how they evolved. There are several ways a fossil can form:

- *Permineralization:* when an organism is buried and its empty spaces fill with mineral-rich groundwater

- *Casts:* when the original remains are completely destroyed and an organism-shaped hole is left in the existing rock

- *Replacement or recrystallization:* when shell or bone is replaced with another mineral

The fossil record provides evidence of *mass extinctions*, which occurred when there was a faster rate of extinction than speciation. It also provides evidence of five ice ages in the Earth's history. *Ice ages* are lengthy periods when the temperature of the Earth's surface and atmosphere are greatly reduced. During these periods, animals that require warmer temperatures for survival can become extinct. *Meteors* are fragments of rock that come from outside of the Earth's atmosphere. A meteor impact can induce a massive change in the atmosphere, also causing mass extinction.

Earth's Bodies of Water

Characteristics and Processes of the Earth's Oceans and Other Bodies of Water

<u>Distribution and Location of the Earth's Water</u>
A *body of water* is any accumulation of water on the Earth's surface. It usually refers to oceans, seas, and lakes, but also includes ponds, wetlands, and puddles. Rivers, streams, and canals are bodies of water that involve the movement of water.

Most bodies of water are naturally occurring geographical features, but they can also be artificially created like lakes created by dams. Saltwater oceans make up 96% of the water on the Earth's surface. Freshwater makes up 2.5% of the remaining water.

<u>Seawater Composition</u>
Seawater is water from a sea or ocean. On average, seawater has a salinity of about 3.5%, meaning every kilogram of seawater has approximately 35 grams of dissolved sodium chloride salt. The average density of saltwater at the surface is 1.025 kg/L, making it denser than pure or freshwater, which has a density of 1.00 kg/L. Because of the dissolved salts, the freezing point of saltwater is also lower than that of pure water; salt water freezes at –2 °C (28 °F). As the concentration of salt increases, the freezing point decreases. Thus, it's more difficult to freeze water from the Dead Sea—a saltwater lake known to have water with such high salinity that swimmers cannot sink.

<u>Coastline Topography and the Topography of Ocean Floor</u>
Topography is the study of natural and artificial features comprising the surface of an area. *Coastlines* are an intermediate area between dry land and the ocean floor. The ground progressively slopes from the dry coastal area to the deepest depth of the ocean floor. At the continental shelf, there's a steep descent of the ocean floor. Although it's often believed that the ocean floor is flat and sandy like a beach, its topography includes mountains, plateaus, and valleys.

Tides, Waves, and Currents

Tides are caused by the pull of the Moon and the Sun. When the Moon is closer in its orbit to the Earth, its gravity pulls the oceans away from the shore. When the distance between the Moon and the Earth is greater, the pull is weaker, and the water on Earth can spread across more land. This relationship creates low and high tides. Waves are influenced by changes in tides as well as the wind. The energy transferred from wind to the top of large bodies of water creates *crests* on the water's surface and *waves* below. Circular movements in the ocean are called *currents*. They result from the Coriolis Effect, which is caused by the Earth's rotation. Currents spin in a clockwise direction above the equator and counterclockwise below the equator.

Estuaries and Barrier Islands

An *estuary* is an area of water located on a coast where a river or stream meets the sea. It's a transitional area that's partially enclosed, has a mix of salty and fresh water, and has calmer water than the open sea. *Barrier islands* are coastal landforms created by waves and tidal action parallel to the mainland coast. They usually occur in chains, and they protect the coastlines and create areas of protected waters where wetlands may flourish.

Islands, Reefs, and Atolls

Islands are land that is completely surrounded by water. *Reefs* are bars of rocky, sandy, or coral material that sit below the surface of water. They may form from sand deposits or erosion of underwater rocks. An *atoll* is a coral reef in the shape of a ring (but not necessarily circular) that encircles a lagoon. In order for an atoll to exist, the rate of its erosion must be slower than the regrowth of the coral that composes the atoll.

Polar Ice, Icebergs, Glaciers

Polar ice is the term for the sheets of ice that cover the poles of a planet. *Icebergs* are large pieces of freshwater ice that break off from glaciers and float in the water. A *glacier* is a persistent body of dense ice that constantly moves because of its own weight. Glaciers form when snow accumulates at a faster rate than it melts over centuries. They form only on land, in contrast to *ice caps*, which can form from sheets of ice in the ocean. When glaciers deform and move due to stresses created by their own weight, they can create crevasses and other large distinguishing land features.

Lakes, Ponds, and Wetlands

Lakes and *ponds* are bodies of water that are surrounded by land. They aren't part of the ocean and don't contain flowing water. Lakes are larger than ponds, but otherwise the two bodies don't have a scientific distinction. *Wetlands* are areas of land saturated by water. They have a unique soil composition and provide a nutrient-dense area for vegetation and aquatic plant growth. They also play a role in water purification and flood control.

Streams, Rivers, and River Deltas

A *river* is a natural flowing waterway usually consisting of freshwater that flows toward an ocean, sea, lake, or another river. Some rivers flow into the ground and become dry instead of reaching another body of water. Small rivers are usually called *streams* or *creeks*. River *deltas* are areas of land formed from the sediment carried by a river and deposited before it enters another body of water. As the river reaches its end, the flow of water slows, and the river loses the power to transport the sediment so it falls out of suspension.

Geysers and Springs

A *spring* is a natural occurrence where water flows from an aquifer to the Earth's surface. A *geyser* is a spring that intermittently and turbulently discharges water. Geysers form only in certain hydrogeological conditions. They require proximity to a volcanic area or magma to provide enough heat to boil or vaporize the water. As hot water and steam accumulate, pressure grows and creates the spraying geyser effect.

Properties of Water that Affect Earth Systems

Water is a chemical compound composed of two hydrogen atoms and one oxygen atom (H_2O) and has many unique properties. In its solid state, water is less dense than its liquid form; therefore, ice floats in water. Water also has a very high heat capacity, allowing it to absorb a high amount of the Sun's energy without getting too hot or evaporating. Its chemical structure makes it a polar compound, meaning one side has a negative charge while the other is positive. This characteristic—along with its ability to form strong intermolecular hydrogen bonds with itself and other molecules—make water an effective solvent for other chemicals.

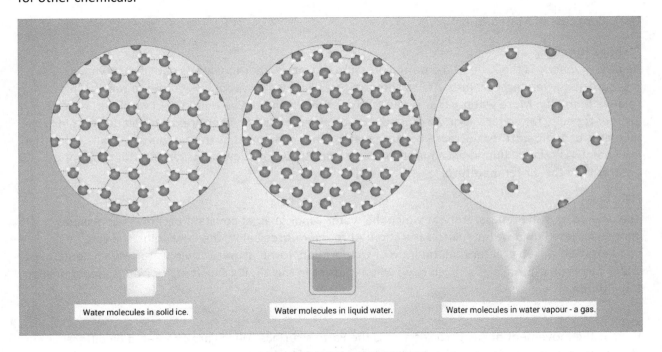

Water molecules in solid ice.　　Water molecules in liquid water.　　Water molecules in water vapour - a gas.

Meteorology and Climate

Basic Structure and Composition of the Earth's Atmosphere

Layers

The Earth's atmospheric layers are determined by their temperatures but are reported by their distance above sea level. Listed from closest to sea level on upward, the levels are:

- Troposphere: sea level to 11 miles above sea level
- Stratosphere: 11 miles to 31 miles above sea level
- Mesosphere: 31 miles to 50 miles above sea level
- Ionosphere: 50 miles to 400 miles above sea level
- Exosphere: 400 miles to 800 miles above sea level

The ionosphere and exosphere are together considered the thermosphere. The ozone layer is in the stratosphere and weather experienced on Earth's surface is a product of factors in the troposphere.

Composition of the Atmosphere

The Earth's atmosphere is composed of gas particles: 78% nitrogen, 21% oxygen, 1% other gases such as argon, and 0.039% carbon dioxide. The atmospheric layers are created by the number of particles in the air and gravity's pull upon them.

Atmospheric Pressure and Temperature

The lower atmospheric levels have higher atmospheric pressures due to the mass of the gas particles located above. The air is less dense (it contains fewer particles per given volume) at higher altitudes. The temperature changes from the bottom to top of each atmospheric layer. The tops of the troposphere and mesosphere are colder than their bottoms, but the reverse is true for the stratosphere and thermosphere. Some of the warmest temperatures are actually found in the thermosphere because of a type of radiation that enters that layer.

Basic Concepts of Meteorology

Relative Humidity

Relative humidity is the ratio of the partial pressure of water vapor to water's equilibrium vapor pressure at a given temperature. At low temperatures, less water vapor is required to reach a high relative humidity. More water vapor is needed to reach a high relative humidity in warm air, which has a greater capacity for water vapor. At ground level or other areas of higher pressure, relative humidity increases as temperatures decrease because water vapor condenses as the temperature falls below the dew point. As relative humidity cannot be greater than 100%, the dew point temperature cannot be greater than the air temperature.

Dew Point

The *dew point* is the temperature at which the water vapor in air at constant barometric pressure condenses into liquid water due to saturation. At temperatures below the dew point, the rate of condensation will be greater than the rate of evaporation, forming more liquid water. When condensed water forms on a surface, it's called *dew*; when it forms in the air, it's called *fog* or *clouds*, depending on the altitude.

Wind

Wind is the movement of gas particles across the Earth's surface. Winds are generated by differences in atmospheric pressure. Air inherently moves from areas of higher pressure to lower pressure, which is what causes wind to occur. Surface friction from geological features, such as mountains or man-made features can decrease wind speed. In meteorology, winds are classified based on their strength, duration, and direction. *Gusts* are short bursts of high-speed wind, *squalls* are strong winds of intermediate duration (around one minute), and winds with a long duration are given names based on their average strength. *Breezes* are the weakest, followed by *gales*, *storms*, and *hurricanes*.

Cloud Types and Formation

Water in the atmosphere can exist as visible masses called *clouds* composed of water droplets, tiny crystals of ice, and various chemicals. Clouds exist primarily in the troposphere. They can be classified based on the altitude at which they occur:

- *High clouds*—between 5,000 and 13,000 meters above sea level
- Cirrus: thin and wispy "mare's tail" appearance

- Cirrocumulus: rows of small puffy pillows
- Cirrostratus: thin sheets that cover the sky
- *Middle clouds*—between 2,000 and 7,000 meters above sea level
- Altocumulus: gray and white and made up of water droplets
- Altostratus: grayish or bluish gray clouds
- *Low clouds*—below 2,000 meters above sea level
- Stratus: gray clouds made of water droplets that can cover the sky
- Stratocumulus: gray and lumpy low-lying clouds
- Nimbostratus: dark gray with uneven bases; typical of rain or snow clouds

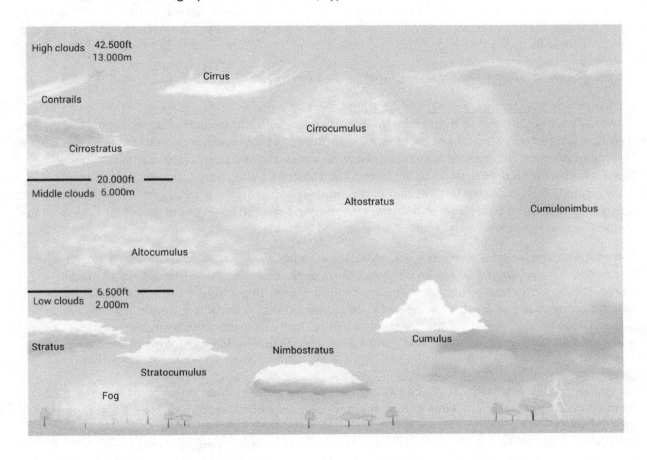

Types of Precipitation

There are three distinct processes by which precipitation occurs. *Convection precipitation* occurs when air rises vertically in a forceful manner, quickly overturning the atmosphere and resulting in heavy precipitation. It's generally more intense and shorter in duration than *stratiform precipitation*, which occurs when large masses of air move over each other. *Orographic precipitation* occurs when moist air is forced upwards over rising terrain, such as a mountain. Most storms are a result of convection precipitation.

Precipitation can fall in liquid or solid phases, as well as any form in between. Liquid precipitation includes rain and drizzle. Frozen precipitation includes snow, sleet, and hail. Intensity is classified by rate of fall or visibility restriction. The forms of precipitation are:

- *Rain*: water vapor that condenses on dust particles in the troposphere until it becomes heavy enough to fall to Earth

- *Sleet*: rain that freezes on its way down; it starts as ice that melts and then freezes again before hitting the ground

- *Hail*: balls of ice thrown up and down several times by turbulent winds, so that more and more water vapor can condense and freeze on the original ice; hail can be as large as golf balls or even baseballs

- *Snow*: loosely packed ice crystals that fall to Earth

Air Masses, Fronts, Storms, and Severe Weather

Air masses are volumes of air defined by their temperature and the amount of water vapor they contain. A *front* is where two air masses of different temperatures and water vapor content meet. Fronts can be the site of extreme weather, such as thunderstorms, which are caused by water particles rubbing against each other. When they do so, electrons are transferred and energy and electrical currents accumulate. When enough energy accumulates, thunder and lightning occur. *Lightning* is a massive electric spark created by a cloud, and *thunder* is the sound created by an expansion of air caused by the sudden increase in pressure and temperature around lightning.

Extreme weather includes tornadoes and hurricanes. *Tornadoes* are created by changing air pressure and winds that can exceed 300 miles per hour. *Hurricanes* occur when warm ocean water quickly evaporates and rises to a colder, low-pressure portion of the atmosphere. Hurricanes, typhoons, and tropical cyclones are all created by the same phenomena but they occur in different regions. *Blizzards* are similar to hurricanes in that they're created by the clash of warm and cold air, but they only occur when cold Arctic air moves toward warmer air. They usually involve large amounts of snow.

Development and Movement of Weather Patterns

A *weather pattern* is weather that's consistent for a period of time. Weather patterns are created by fronts. A *cold front* is created when two air masses collide in a high-pressure system. A *warm front* is created when a low-pressure system results from the collision of two air masses; they are usually warmer and less dense than high-pressure systems. When a cold front enters an area, the air from the warm front is forced upwards. The temperature of the warm front's air decreases, condenses, and often creates clouds and precipitation. When a warm front moves into an area, the warm air moves slowly upwards at an angle. Clouds and precipitation form, but the precipitation generally lasts longer because of how slowly the air moves.

Major Factors that Affect Climate and Seasons

Effects of Latitude, Geographical Location, and Elevation

The climate and seasons of different geographical areas are primarily dictated by their sunlight exposure. Because the Earth rotates on a tilted axis while travelling around the Sun, different latitudes get different amounts of direct sunlight throughout the year, creating different climates. Polar regions experience the greatest variation, with long periods of limited or no sunlight in the winter and up to 24 hours of daylight in the summer. Equatorial regions experience the least variance in direct sunlight exposure. Coastal areas experience breezes in the summer as cooler ocean air moves ashore, while areas southeast of the Great Lakes can get "lake effect" snow in the winter, as cold air travels over the warmer water and creates snow on land. Mountains are often seen with snow in the spring and fall. Their high elevation causes mountaintops to stay cold. The air around the mountaintop is also cold and holds less water vapor than air at sea level. As the water vapor condenses, it creates snow.

Effects of Atmospheric Circulation

Global winds are patterns of wind circulation and they have a major influence on global weather and climate. They help influence temperature and precipitation by carrying heat and water vapor around the Earth. These winds are driven by the uneven heating between the polar and equatorial regions created by the Sun. Cold air from the polar regions sinks and moves toward the equator, while the warm air from the equator rises and moves toward the poles. The other factor driving global winds is the *Coriolis Effect*. As air moves from the North Pole to the equator, the Earth's rotation makes it seem as if the wind is also moving to the right, or westbound, and eastbound from South Pole to equator.

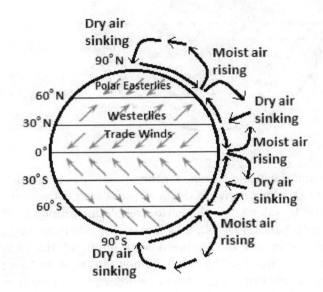

Global wind patterns are given names based on which direction they blow. There are three major wind patterns in each hemisphere. Notice the image above diagramming the movement of warm (dry) air and moist (cold) air.

Trade winds—easterly surface winds found in the troposphere near the equator—blow predominantly from the northeast in the Northern Hemisphere and from the southeast in the Southern Hemisphere. These winds direct the tropical storms that develop over the Atlantic, Pacific, and Indian Oceans and land in North America, Southeast Asia, and eastern Africa, respectively. *Jet streams* are westerly winds that follow a narrow, meandering path. The two strongest jet streams are the polar jets and the subtropical jets. In the Northern Hemisphere, the polar jet flows over the middle of North America, Europe, and Asia, while in the Southern Hemisphere, it circles Antarctica.

Effects of Ocean Circulation

Ocean currents are similar to global winds because winds influence how the oceans move. Ocean currents are created by warm water moving from the equator towards the poles while cold water travels from the poles to the equator. The warm water can increase precipitation in an area because it evaporates faster than the colder water.

<u>Characteristics and Locations of Climate Zones</u>

Climate zones are created by the Earth's tilt as it travels around the Sun. These zones are delineated by the equator and four other special latitudinal lines: the Tropic of Cancer or Northern Tropic at 23.5° North; the Tropic of Capricorn or Southern Tropic at 23.5° South; the Arctic Circle at 66.5° North; and the Antarctic Circle at 66.5° South. The areas between these lines of latitude represent different climate zones. Tropical climates are hot and wet, like rainforests, and tend to have abundant plant and animal life, while polar climates are cold and usually have little plant and animal life. Temperate zones can vary and experience the four seasons.

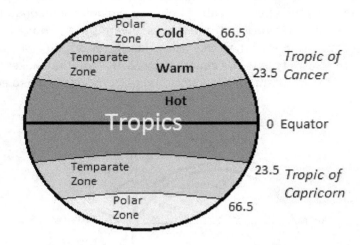

<u>Effect of the Tilt of the Earth's Axis on Seasons</u>

In addition to the equator and the prime meridian, other major lines of latitude and longitude divide the world into regions relative to the direct rays of the Sun. These lines correspond with the Earth's 23.5-degree tilt, and are responsible—along with the Earth's revolution around the Sun—for the seasons. For example, the Northern Hemisphere is tilted directly toward the Sun from June 22 to September 23, which creates the summer. Conversely, the Southern Hemisphere is tilted away from the Sun and experiences winter during those months. The area between the Tropic of Cancer and the Tropic of Capricorn tends to be warmer and experiences fewer variations in seasonal temperatures because it's constantly subject to the direct rays of the Sun, no matter which direction the Earth is tilted.

The area between the Tropic of Cancer and the Arctic Circle, which is at 66.5° North, and the Antarctic Circle, which is at 66.5° South, is where most of Earth's population resides and is called the *middle latitudes*. Here, the seasons are more pronounced, and milder temperatures generally prevail. When the Sun's direct rays are over the equator, it's known as an *equinox*, and day and night are almost equal throughout the world. Equinoxes occur twice a year: the fall, or autumnal equinox, occurs on September 22, while the spring equinox occurs on March 20.

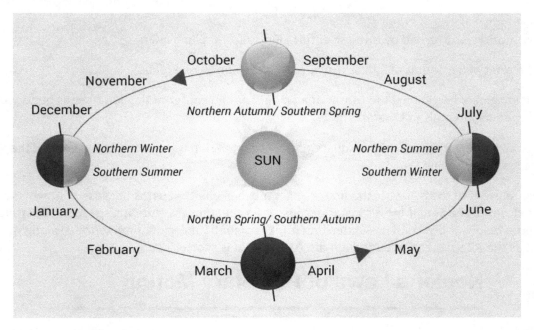

Effects of Natural Phenomena
Natural phenomena can have a sizeable impact on climate and weather. Chemicals released from volcanic eruptions can fall back to Earth in acid rain. In addition, large amounts of carbon dioxide released into the atmosphere can warm the climate. Carbon dioxide creates the *greenhouse effect* by trapping solar energy from sunlight reflected off the Earth's surface within the atmosphere. The amount of solar radiation emitted from the Sun varies and has recently been discovered to be cyclical.

El Niño and La Niña
El Niño and *La Niña* are terms for severe weather anomalies associated with torrential rainfall in the Pacific coastal regions, mainly in North and South America. These events occur irregularly every few years, usually around December, and are caused by a band of warm ocean water that accumulates in the central Pacific Ocean around the equator. The warm water changes the wind patterns over the Pacific and stops cold water from rising toward the American coastlines. The rise in ocean temperature also leads to increased evaporation and rain. These events are split into two phases—a warm, beginning phase called El Niño and a cool end phase called La Niña.

Astronomy

Major Features of the Solar System

Structure of the Solar System
The *solar system* is an elliptical planetary system with a large sun in the center that provides gravitational pull on the planets. It was formed 4.568 billion years ago from the gravitational collapse of a region within a giant molecular cloud that likely birthed other suns. This region of collapse is called a *pre-solar nebula*. As it started to collapse in the center, the nebula accumulated more energy and became hotter and heavier, providing more gravitational energy to the rest of the cloud, eventually becoming the Sun. The planets likely formed in a similar fashion, starting as small clumps called

protoplanets that revolved around the Sun and then smashed together to form larger planets and, eventually, the Solar System seen today.

Laws of Motion

Planetary motion is governed by three scientific laws called Kepler's laws:

1. The orbit of a planet is elliptical in shape, with the Sun as one focus.

2. An imaginary line joining the center of a planet and the center of the Sun sweeps out equal areas during equal intervals of time.

3. For all planets, the ratio of the square of the orbital period is the same as the cube of the average distance from the Sun.

The most relevant of these laws is the first. Planets move in elliptical paths because of gravity; when a planet is closer to the Sun, it moves faster because it has built up gravitational speed. As illustrated in the diagram below, the second law states that it takes planet 1 the same time to travel along the A1 segment as the A2 segment, even though the A2 segment is shorter.

Kepler's Laws of Planetary Motion

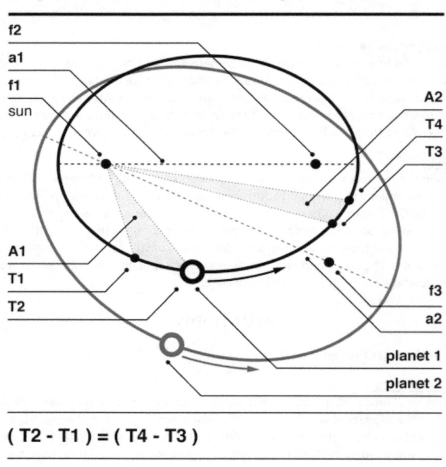

$$(T2 - T1) = (T4 - T3)$$

$$\Delta\ TA1 = \Delta\ TA2$$

Characteristics of the Sun, Moon, and Planets

The Sun is comprised mainly of hydrogen and helium. Metals make up only about 2% of its total mass. The Sun is 1.3 million kilometers wide, weighs 1.989×10^{30} kilograms, and has temperatures of 5,800 Kelvin (9980 °F) on the surface and 15,600,000 Kelvin (28 million °F) at the core. The Sun's enormous size and gravity give it the ability to provide sunlight. The gravity of the Sun compresses hydrogen and helium atoms together through nuclear fusion and releases energy and light.

The Moon has a distinct core, mantle, and crust. It has elevations and craters created by impacts with large objects in the solar system. The Moon makes a complete orbit around the Earth every 27.3 days. It's relatively large compared to other moons in the Solar System, with a diameter one-quarter of the Earth and a mass 1/81 of the Earth.

The eight planets of the Solar System are divided into four inner (or terrestrial) planets and four outer (or Jovian) planets. In general, terrestrial planets are small, and Jovian planets are large and gaseous. The planets in the Solar System are listed below from nearest to farthest from the Sun:

- Mercury: the smallest planet in the Solar System; it only takes about 88 days to completely orbit the Sun.

- Venus: around the same size, composition, and gravity as Earth and orbits the Sun every 225 days.

- Earth: the only known planet with life

- Mars: called the Red Planet due to iron oxide on the surface; takes around 365 days to complete its orbit

- Jupiter: the largest planet in the system; made up of mainly hydrogen and helium

- Saturn: mainly composed of hydrogen and helium along with other trace elements; has 61 moons; has beautiful rings, which may be remnants of destroyed moons

- Uranus: the coldest planet in the system, with temperatures as low as -224.2 °Celsius (-371.56 °F)

- Neptune: the last and third-largest planet; also, the second-coldest planet

Asteroids, Meteoroids, Comets, and Dwarf/Minor Planets

Several other bodies travel through the universe. *Asteroids* are orbiting bodies composed of minerals and rock. They're also known as *minor planets*—a term given to any astronomical object in orbit around the Sun that doesn't resemble a planet or a comet. *Meteoroids* are mini-asteroids with no specific orbiting pattern. *Meteors* are meteoroids that have entered the Earth's atmosphere and started melting from contact with greenhouse gases. *Meteorites* are meteors that have landed on Earth. *Comets* are composed of dust and ice and look like a comma with a tail from the melting ice as they streak across the sky.

Theories of Origin of the Solar System

One theory of the origins of the Solar System is the *nebular hypothesis*, which posits that the Solar System was formed by clouds of extremely hot gas called a *nebula*. As the nebula gases cooled, they became smaller and started rotating. Rings of the nebula left behind during rotation eventually condensed into planets and their satellites. The remaining nebula formed the Sun.

Another theory of the Solar System's development is the *planetesimal hypothesis*. This theory proposes that planets formed from cosmic dust grains that collided and stuck together to form larger and larger bodies. The larger bodies attracted each other, growing into moon-sized protoplanets and eventually planets.

Interactions of the Earth-Moon-Sun System

The Earth's Rotation and Orbital Revolution Around the Sun
Besides revolving around the Sun, the Earth also spins like a top. It takes one day for the Earth to complete a full spin, or rotation. The same is true for other planets, except that their "days" may be shorter or longer. One Earth day is about 24 hours, while one Jupiter day is only about nine Earth hours, and a Venus day is about 241 Earth days. Night occurs in areas that face away from the Sun, so one side of the planet experiences daylight and the other experiences night. This phenomenon is the reason that the Earth is divided into time zones. The concept of time zones was created to provide people around the world with a uniform standard time, so the Sun would rise around 7:00 AM, regardless of location.

Effect on Seasons
The Earth's tilted axis creates the seasons. When Earth is tilted toward the Sun, the Northern Hemisphere experiences summer while the Southern Hemisphere has winter—and vice versa. As the Earth rotates, the distribution of direct sunlight slowly changes, explaining how the seasons gradually change.

Phases of the Moon
The Moon goes through two phases as it revolves around Earth: waxing and waning. Each phase lasts about two weeks:

- Waxing—the right side of the Moon is illuminated
- New moon (dark): the Moon rises and sets with the Sun
- Crescent: a tiny sliver of illumination on the right
- First quarter: the right half the Moon is illuminated
- Gibbous: more than half of the Moon is illuminated
- Full moon: the Moon rises at sunset and sets at sunrise
- Waning—the left side of the Moon is illuminated
- Gibbous: more than half is illuminated, only here it is the left side that is illuminated
- Last quarter: the left half of the Moon is illuminated
- Crescent: a tiny sliver of illumination on the left
- New moon (dark)—the Moon rises and sets with the Sun

Effect on Tides
Although the Earth is much larger, the Moon still has a significant gravitational force that pulls on Earth's oceans. At its closest to Earth, the Moon's gravitation pull is greatest and creates high tide. The opposite is true when the Moon is farthest from the Earth: less pull creates low tide.

Solar and Lunar Eclipses
Eclipses occur when the Earth, the Sun, and the Moon are all in line. If the three bodies are perfectly aligned, a total eclipse occurs; otherwise, it's only a partial eclipse. A *solar eclipse* occurs when the Moon

is between the Earth and the Sun, blocking sunlight from reaching the Earth. A *lunar eclipse* occurs when the Earth interferes with the Sun's light reflecting off the full moon. The Earth casts a shadow on the Moon, but the particles of the Earth's atmosphere refract the light, so some light reaches the Moon, causing it to look yellow, brown, or red.

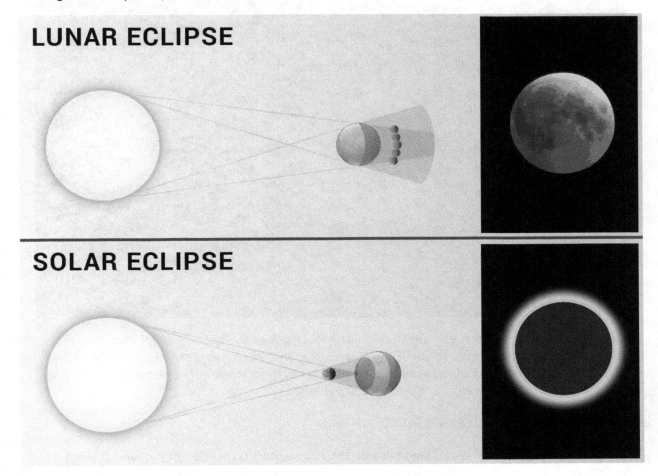

LUNAR ECLIPSE

SOLAR ECLIPSE

Time Zones

Longitudinal, or vertical, lines determine how far east or west different regions are from each other. These lines, also known as *meridians,* are the basis for time zones, which allocate different times to regions depending on their position eastward and westward of the prime meridian.

Effect of Solar Wind on the Earth

Solar winds are streams of charged particles emitted by the Sun, consisting of mostly electrons, protons, and alpha particles. The Earth is largely protected from solar winds by its magnetic field. However, the winds can still be observed, as they create phenomena like the beautiful Northern Lights (or Aurora Borealis).

Major Features of the Universe

Galaxies

Galaxies are clusters of stars, rocks, ice, and space dust. Like everything else in space, the exact number of galaxies is unknown, but there could be as many as a hundred billion. There are three types of galaxies: spiral, elliptical, and irregular. Most galaxies are *spiral galaxies*; they have a large, central galactic bulge made up of a cluster of older stars. They look like a disk with spinning arms. *Elliptical galaxies* are groups of stars with no pattern of rotation. They can be spherical or extremely elongated, and they don't have arms. *Irregular galaxies* vary significantly in size and shape.

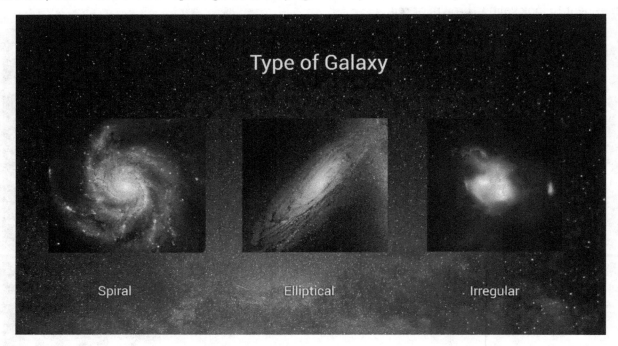

To say that galaxies are large is an understatement. Most galaxies are 1,000 to 100,000 parsecs in diameter, with one *parsec* equal to about 19 trillion miles. The Milky Way is the galaxy that contains Earth's Solar System. It's one of the smaller galaxies that has been studied. The diameter of the Milky Way is estimated to be between 31,000 to 55,000 parsecs.

<u>Characteristics of Stars and Their Life Cycles</u>
Life Cycle of Stars
All stars are formed from nebulae. Depending on their mass, stars take different pathways during their evolution. Low- and medium-mass stars start as nebulae and then become red giants and white dwarfs. High-mass stars become red supergiants, supernovas, and then either neutron stars or black holes. Official stars are born as red dwarves because they have plentiful amounts of gas—mainly hydrogen—to undergo nuclear fusion. Red dwarves mature into white dwarves before expending their hydrogen fuel source. When the fuel is spent, it creates a burst of energy that expands the star into a red giant. Red giants eventually condense to form white dwarves, which is the final stage of a star's life.

Stars that undergo nuclear fusion and energy expenditure extremely quickly can burst in violent explosions called *supernovas*. These bursts can release as much energy in a few seconds as the Sun can release in its entire lifetime. The particles from the explosion then condense into the smallest type of star—a neutron star—and eventually form a *black hole*, which has such a high amount of gravity that not even light energy can escape. The Sun is currently a red dwarf, early in its life cycle.

Color, Temperature, Apparent Brightness, Absolute Brightness, and Luminosity
The color of a star depends on its surface temperature. Stars with cooler surfaces emit red light, while the hottest stars give off blue light. Stars with temperatures between these extremes, such as the Sun, emit white light. The *apparent brightness* of a star is a measure of how bright a star appears to an observer on the Earth. The *absolute brightness* is a measure of the intrinsic brightness of a star and is

measured at a distance of exactly 10 parsecs away. The *luminosity* of a star is the amount of light emitted from its surface.

Hertzsprung-Russell Diagrams
Hertzsprung-Russell diagrams are scatterplots that show the relationship of a star's brightness and temperature, or color. The general layout shows stars of greater luminosity toward the top of the diagram. Stars with higher surface temperatures appear toward the left side of the diagram. The diagonal area from the top-left of the diagram to the bottom-right is called the *main sequence*. Stars may or may not follow the main sequence during their evolutionary period.

Dark Matter
Dark matter is an unidentified type of matter that comprises approximately 27% of the mass and energy in the observable universe. As the name suggests, dark matter is so dense and small that it doesn't emit or interact with electromagnetic radiation, such as light, making it electromagnetically invisible. Although dark matter has never been directly observed, its existence and properties can be inferred from its gravitational effects on visible objects as well as the cosmic microwave background. Patterns of movement have been observed in visible objects that would only be possible if dark matter exerted a gravitational pull.

Theories About the Origin of the Universe
The *Big Bang theory* is the most plausible cosmological model for the origin of the universe. It theorizes that the universe expanded from a high-density and high-temperature state. The theory offers comprehensive explanations for a wide range of astronomical phenomena, such as the cosmic microwave background and Hubble's Law. From detailed measurements of the expansion rate of the universe, it's estimated that the Big Bang occurred approximately 13.8 billion years ago, which is considered the age of the universe. The theory states that after the initial expansion, the universe cooled enough for subatomic particles and atoms to form and aggregate into giant clouds. These clouds coalesced through gravity and formed the stars and galaxies. If this theory holds true, it's predicted that the universe will reach a point where it will stop expanding and start to pull back toward the center due to gravity.

Contributions of Space Exploration and Technology to our Understanding of the Universe

Remote Sensing Devices
Scientists and astronomers use satellites and other technology to explore the universe because humans cannot yet safely travel far into space. The *telescope* allows observation beyond what the naked eye can see. With information from the Planck satellite, astronomers were able to determine that the observable universe is actually smaller than earlier believed; they estimated that the universe is smaller by 320 million light years, giving it a total radius of 45.34 billion light years. *Astronomical spectroscopy* uses spectroscopy techniques to measure visible light and radiation from stars and other hot celestial objects. This information allows scientists to determine the physical properties of stars that would otherwise be impossible to measure, including chemical composition, temperature, density, and mass.

Search for Water and Life on Other Planets
Even the smallest microorganisms on Earth cannot live without liquid water. Water is essential to life, which is why scientists believe the search for water is the best way to find life on other planets. Water can be found throughout the universe in the form of ice. For example, some of Saturn's rings are composed of ice, and comets streaking through the sky release ice particles through their tails. Until recently, it was believed that the Earth was the only place with liquid water. Through the use of

satellites and telescopes, astronomers have discovered that two of Jupiter's moons—Europa and Callisto—may contain liquid water below their surfaces.

Practice Questions

1. Which rock is formed from cooling magma underneath the Earth's surface?
    a. Extrusive sedimentary rocks
    b. Sedimentary rocks
    c. Igneous rocks
    d. Metamorphic rocks

2. Pure gold is an example of which class of mineral?
    a. Carbonate
    b. Silicates
    c. Elements
    d. Oxides

3. Water that has seeped into rock cracks and freezes will most likely result in what process?
    a. Chemical weathering
    b. Mechanical weathering
    c. Erosion
    d. Deposition

4. Which soil is the least permeable to water?
    a. Pure sand
    b. Pure silt
    c. Pure clay
    d. Loam

5. Which of the Earth's layers is thickest?
    a. The crust
    b. The shell
    c. The mantle
    d. The inner core

6. Which of the following is true regarding the Earth's southern geomagnetic pole?
    a. It's always around the same area
    b. It's near the North Pole
    c. It's near the South Pole
    d. It never moves

7. What is the process called in which a tectonic plate moves over another plate?
    a. Fault
    b. Diversion
    c. Subduction
    d. Drift

8. What is transpiration?
    a. Evaporation from moving water
    b. Evaporation from plant life
    c. Movement of water through the ground
    d. Precipitation that falls on trees

9. Absolute dating involves which of the following?
    a. Measuring radioactive decay
    b. Comparing rock stratification
    c. Fossil location
    d. Fossil record

10. Which of the following will freeze last?
    a. Freshwater from a pond
    b. Pure water
    c. Seawater from the Pacific Ocean
    d. Seawater from the Dead Sea

11. Which of the following is true of glaciers?
    a. They form in water.
    b. They float.
    c. They form on land.
    d. They are formed from icebergs.

12. Where do geysers get the energy to spray water?
    a. From magma
    b. From the Sun
    c. From springs
    d. From rivers

13. Which of the following is most abundant in the Earth's atmosphere?
    a. Carbon dioxide
    b. Oxygen
    c. Nitrogen
    d. Water

14. Dew point is a measure of which of the following?
        I. Pressure
        II. Temperature at which water vapor condenses
        III. Temperature at which water evaporates
    a. I and III
    b. I and II
    c. II and III
    d. All the above

15. The Coriolis Effect is created by which of the following?
    a. Wind
    b. Earth's rotation
    c. Earth's axis
    d. Mountains

16. Dark storm clouds are usually located where?
    a. Between 5,000 and 13,000 meters above sea level
    b. Between 2,000 and 7,000 meters above sea level
    c. Below 2,000 meters above sea level
    d. Outer space

17. Kepler's laws help explain which of the following?
    a. How the Earth moves around the Sun
    b. How water moves around the Earth
    c. How sunlight moves through space
    d. How air moves around the Earth

18. Which of the following best describes this moon phase?

    a. Gibbous
    b. Waxing
    c. Waning
    d. Crescent

19. The Big Bang theory helps explain which of the following?
    a. The expanding universe
    b. Dark matter
    c. Life
    d. Gravity

20. Currently, water can be found where?
    a. On the Earth
    b. Around Saturn
    c. On Jupiter's moons
    d. All of the above

Answers and Explanations

1. C: Igneous rocks are formed from the cooling of magma, both on and below the Earth's surface, which are classified as extrusive and intrusive, respectively. Sedimentary rocks are formed from deposition and cementation on the surface, and metamorphic rocks are formed from the transformation of sedimentary or igneous rocks through heat and pressure.

2. C: Elements are minerals formed by elements that occur naturally and aren't combined with other elements or substances. This group contains metals such as gold and nickel.

3. B: Freezing water expands because ice is less dense than liquid water. This expansion can break up solid rocks, which describes a form of mechanical weathering. Chemical weathering occurs when water dissolves rocks. Erosion is the movement of broken rock, and deposition is the process of laying down rocks from erosion.

4. C: Pure clay has small particles that pack together tightly and are impermeable to water. Sand is the least permeable type of soil because it has the largest grains. Loam is a combination of all three types of soil in relatively equal proportions.

5. C: The mantle is the Earth's thickest layer; it holds most of the Earth's material. The crust is thin, and the inner core is also small compared to the mantle. There is no such thing as Earth's shell.

6. B: Earth's southern geomagnetic pole is located near Greenland. It constantly moves around the same area, but it can intermittently flip or reverse every 100,000 years or so.

7. C: Subduction occurs when one plate is pushed down by another. A fault is where two plates meet. Diversion occurs when two plates move apart. Drift isn't a term used with tectonic plates.

8. B: Transpiration is water that evaporates from pores in plants called stomata. Evaporation of moving water is still called evaporation. Infiltration is the process of water moving into the ground, and precipitation that falls on trees is called canopy interception.

9. A: Absolute dating involves measuring radioactive decay of elements such as carbon-14 trapped in rocks or minerals and using the known rate of decay to determine how much time has passed. Another element used is uranium-lead, which allows dating for some of the oldest rocks on the Earth.

10. D: Water with a higher salinity has more dissolved salt and a lower freezing point. Water from the Dead Sea has the highest salinity of the answer choices.

11. C: Glaciers are formed only on land and constantly move because of their own weight. Icebergs are formed from glaciers and float.

12. A: Geysers get their energy from magma within the Earth. The magma heats up water within the geyser until enough pressure builds up to create a geyser's spray.

13. C: Nitrogen is the most abundant element in the atmosphere at 78%. Carbon dioxide and water don't make up a large percentage. Oxygen makes up only 21% of the atmosphere.

14. C: The dew point is the temperature at which the water vapor in a sample of air at constant barometric pressure condenses into water at the same rate at which it evaporates. It isn't a measure of pressure.

15. B: The Coriolis Effect is created by Earth's rotation. As wind moves toward the equator, the Earth's rotation also makes the wind move to the west. The Earth's axis and mountains don't play a part in the Coriolis Effect.

16. C: Dark storm clouds are considered nimbostratus clouds, which are located below 2,000 meters above sea level. There are no atmospheric clouds in outer space.

17. A: Kepler's laws are:

a. The orbit of a planet is elliptical in shape, with the Sun as one focus.
b. An imaginary line joining the center of a planet and the center of the Sun sweeps out equal areas during equal intervals of time.
c. The ratio of the square of the orbital period to the cube of the average distance from the Sun is the same for all planets.

These laws explain planetary motion created by gravity, such as the Earth's movement around the Sun. They don't have anything to do with how water, air, or sunlight move.

18. C: When the left side of the Moon is illuminated, as it is in the given figure, it's in the waning phase. In contrast, when the right side of the Moon is illuminated, it's in its waxing phase. Gibbous describes a moon that's more than half-illuminated, and a crescent is less than half-illuminated.

19. A: The Big Bang theory explains how the universe was created from a large explosion, resulting in an expanding cloud of cosmic dust that clumped together to form stars and planets. Dark matter and life are found within the universe, and gravity is a universal law that helps explain how the Big Bang occurred.

20. D: Ice (solid water) can be found in Saturn's rings. Liquid water may have recently been discovered on Jupiter's moons Europa and Callisto.

Science, Technology, and Society

Impact of Science and Technology on the Environment and Society

Advances in science and technology can have both positive and negative impacts on the environment and society. Often, new discoveries and technologies make daily living more convenient for the average person. However, these advancements initially require extra natural resources and the long-term effects on society take time to be fully understood. It's also important to note that many scientific and technological advancements focus on mitigating, or even eliminating, longstanding environmental and societal concerns.

Air and Water Pollution

Air and water are vital to human existence. Clean air and potable water greatly impact human health outcomes. As countries develop and become more industrialized, pollution is inevitable. In the United States, the Industrial Revolution, which shifted the economy's focus from agricultural practices to manufacturing, greatly increased air, water, and soil pollution. This occurred because factories burned more coal to operate, leading to increased levels of *smog* (a type of hazy air resulting from the presence of smoke, sulfur oxides, nitrogen oxides, and/or additional hazardous organic compounds) and the presence of *acid rain* (rain that is acidic as a result of air pollution and consequently harms trees, bodies of water, and animals when it falls). Additionally, factories often disposed of waste in the most convenient manner possible—usually by dumping it into bodies of water often used for drinking water. By the middle of the 20th century, both the United States and England had experienced deadly smog events that had resulted in the deaths and sickness of thousands of citizens. These events spurred environmental movements in the 1960s, and the United States passed the *Clean Air Act* in 1970 to combat environmental hazards resulting from air pollution. Currently, many companies focus on the development and implementation of "clean" technologies to manage these issues. The introduction of battery-operated vehicles intended to reduce the country's production of automotive emissions is just one example.

Climate Change and Greenhouse Gases

Greenhouse gases in the Earth's atmosphere include water vapor, carbon dioxide, methane, nitrous oxide, and *chlorofluorocarbons (CFCs)*, which trap heat between the surface of the Earth and the Earth's lowest atmospheric layer, the troposphere. The increase of these gases leads to warming or cooling trends that cause unpredictable or unprecedented meteorological shifts. These shifts can cause natural disasters, affect plant and animal life, and dramatically impact human health. *Water vapor* is a naturally found gas, but as the Earth's temperature rises, the presence of water vapor increases; as water vapor increases, the Earth's temperature rises. This creates a somewhat undesirable loop. *Carbon dioxide* is produced through natural causes, such as volcanic eruptions, but also is greatly affected by human activities, such as burning fossil fuels. A significant increase in the presence of atmospheric carbon dioxide has been noted since the Industrial Revolution; this is important as carbon dioxide is considered the most significant influencer of climate change on Earth. *Methane* is produced primarily from animal and agriculture waste and landfill waste. *Nitrous oxide* is primarily produced from the use of fertilizers and fossil fuels. CFCs are completely synthetic and were previously commonly found in aerosol and other high pressure containers; however, after being linked to ozone layer depletion, they have been stringently regulated internationally and are now in limited use. Scientists have stated that the climate shifts recorded since the Industrial Revolution cannot be attributed to natural causes alone, as the patterns do not follow those of climate shifts that took place prior to the Industrial Revolution.

Natural Greenhouse Effect vs. Human Influence

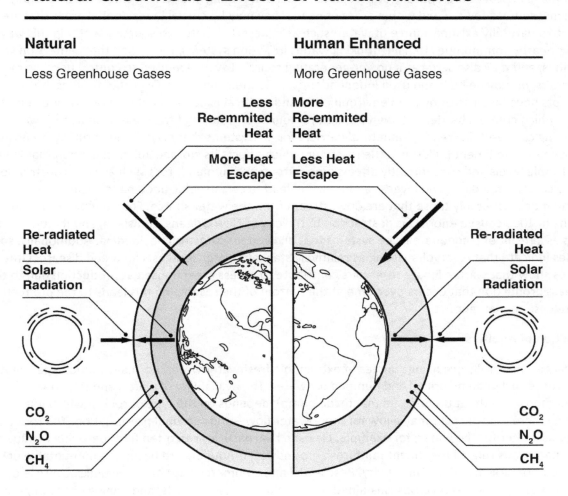

Irrigation

Irrigation refers to a systematic watering method, most pertinent to the agriculture and landscaping industries. It is not the only method of watering used in agricultural practices (some farmers and landscapers do utilize natural rainfall alone), but it is the primary method in which humans can control how to best utilize their most reliable water source for agricultural purposes. Irrigation systems can also be used in conjunction with a community's sewage and drainage system. There are multiple methods of irrigation, although they all have the same goal of supplying crops with a sufficient amount of water. Surface irrigation is the most commonly utilized method of irrigation, functioning by allowing water to freely flow across the desired area and naturally seeping into the soil below. Localized irrigation distributes water through piping and sprays directly onto a plant. An example is a residential sprinkler system that waters an entire lawn through in-ground nozzles, or a drip irrigation system that distributes water using low-flow pressure systems. Subsurface irrigation systems are underground and concentrate water at the root of a plant. Some methods of localized irrigation also combine fertilizer into the watering system.

Reservoirs and Levees

Reservoirs and *levees* are typically utilized as a means of directing and storing water from naturally occurring sources toward and within areas of need. They may be crucial in residential areas that are not close to a naturally existing source of water, such as in desert climates. Resourcing water in this way allows nearby communities to have drinking water, irrigation systems, recreation that centers on water activities, and may also serve as a power-generating source. Levees are used to control flooding of reservoirs, or may be built and used independently in flood-prone areas. Over the decades, both concepts have faced scrutiny from environmental and political experts. Creating a reservoir often utilizes dams, which create a barrier between the natural source of water and the created source of water. Damming can result in creating unnatural barriers for ecosystems that exist in the naturally occurring water source; sediment build-up in the reservoir, which affects its storage abilities; erosion that lowers water table levels and consequently affects crop output; and human errors such as poor construction. Poorly constructed dams and levees can break and lead to catastrophic flooding for nearby communities, especially those that are downstream from the water source. For example, Hurricane Katrina in 2005 caused enormous destruction to the city of New Orleans, Louisiana, and its surrounding areas as a result of inadequate levee systems that allowed for catastrophic flooding. Additionally, some studies indicate that reservoirs, acting as relatively stagnant water sources, can breed disease. Other studies show that warm-climate reservoirs contribute to excess greenhouse gas production due to the biomass production that occurs over time at the bottom of the reservoirs; this leads to the production and release of methane.

Depletion of Aquifers

Aquifers are naturally occurring sources of extractable freshwater water, normally found in permeable rock. These rocks can be drilled and pumped for water. The availability of water, and if it flows autonomously (without the use of a manmade pump), depends on the type of rock in which it is stored—more porous rocks may allow for more water flow—and seasonal precipitation. The rock also serves as a filter for the water; for example, clay and coal particles can often filter pesticide residue and other hazardous run-off that might taint fresh groundwater. Aquifers are becoming non-potable or depleted primarily from human activity. Residential and commercial use of septic tanks, overuse of fertilizers and pesticides on crops, sustained pumping along ocean coasts, and mining either degrade the quality of the water by allowing hazardous contaminants (such as waste or saltwater) to enter it, or by exposing the water to air and allowing it to evaporate. Depletion occurs when pumping occurs faster than the rocks can replenish their water stores. With exponential population growth, aquifer water is being used at a rate at which it cannot be replenished quickly enough.

Ozone Layer Depletion

Located in the stratosphere, the *ozone layer* protects the Earth from excessive *ultraviolet B (UVB)* ray exposure. The last century has shown signification depletion of the ozone layer, especially over Antarctica; this region is known as the *ozone hole*, missing almost 70% of its ozone layer. Chlorine molecules are especially harmful to ozone molecules. CFCs have been a major contributor to the ozone layer's depletion due to their high concentration of chlorine molecules. Almost all CFC production was a result of industrialization and human activity. In 1996, most CFC production was banned; however, it is expected that atmospheric chlorine levels will remain high for the next couple of decades. Additionally, other effects of climate change may prevent the stratosphere from ever reaching the gas composition that existed before CFCs were utilized. While ozone depletion does not contribute to global warming directly, its impact on human health and disease is significant. The consequent increase in UVB exposure is linked to skin cancer in people, and ecosystem and food source disruption in animals. The effect on plants can lead to plant loss, which can indirectly impact the greenhouse effect, global warming, climate change, and human health.

Loss of Biodiversity

Biodiversity refers to the varied number of species on Earth—ranging from humans, to fish, to plants— and the way ecosystems are built within them. The biodiversity of an area strongly influences its air and soil quality, its energy availability, and how well its community thrives. Natural resources are currently being expended faster rate than they can be replaced, which is resulting in the extinction of species. As all species are interconnected in some way, the loss of an entire species can detrimentally impact the interactions and existence of other species. For example, if a particular animal feeds primarily on a plant species that becomes extinct, the animal species will have to radically change its feeding behaviors or it becomes prone to extinction. Decreasing supplies of water can impact the existence of plant and animal species as well, which, in turn, may affect how and what humans eat and grow. Plants are crucial to providing oxygen and reducing carbon dioxide—a greenhouse gas—on Earth. Additionally, many plants serve as ingredient sources in medicines; loss of plant life affects not only potential food sources but also medicinal sources. Overpopulation is likely the biggest threat to biodiversity, due to the inherent competing needs for land, water, and food production, as well as the risks of excess waste and pollution.

Space Exploration

Space, found beyond the Earth's atmosphere, has been a point of fascination for millennia. The development of rockets finally allowed for physical space exploration in the 1950s, with the intention of expanding knowledge in the fields of astronomy and physics. The 1950s were a time of competition between countries, as a number of countries attempted to pioneer the first space exploration. The Soviet Union launched the first orbiting satellite in 1957, and the United States succeeded in the first manned moon landing in 1969. China also sent manned missions to space in the 2000s. Additionally, satellites have been launched with the purpose of observing the Earth, serving as communication and navigation beacons, optimizing radio and television function, and relaying weather currently orbit the Earth. Present day has shifted some focus to exploring Mars and the potential for creating livable environments outside of the Earth. Some believe that limiting human existence to Earth only will ultimately lead to extinction as resources dwindle. Currently, the International Space Station is the only inhabitable, permanent structure outside of Earth and has been in use for almost two decades. The National Aeronautics and Space Administration (NASA) announced its intention to build a Moon station by 2024. There is also a focus on artificial intelligence and using automated, fully-functional, yet unmanned missions into deep space to conduct further exploration and research. However, much remains to be discovered about living in space. Conditions in space are harsh to human physiology, and no feasible long-term means of mitigating such effects yet exist.

Waste Disposal and Landfills

Waste disposal is a serious human concern. Waste production has almost doubled in the United States in the last 50 years, with the average household producing over 6,000 pounds of trash per year. Over half of that waste is disposed of in man-made sites in the Earth's ground. Piling (and even burying) trash is an ancient tradition. *Dumps* are open pits of trash, susceptible to rot, stench, and animal infestations. *Landfills* are designed structures intended to create a distinct boundary between the trash and the Earth. This boundary may be made of plastic, or with clay and soil. These structures try to prevent contamination of aquifers and crop soil. As waste breaks down in a landfill, methane is released into the air. Environmental groups and government regulations are pushing lifestyle changes and new technologies to reduce human trash generation. These include repurposing waste, extracting valuable materials from waste, turning waste into a renewable energy source, and advocating green behaviors such as using reusable grocery bags, using fewer plastic goods, and having *compost bins* at home. Many items in landfills could be disposed of in compost bins. These are composed of organic materials that decay quickly, such as food rinds and plant detritus. Once decayed, this material can be used to enrich soil and plant life, limit erosion, and even retain extra groundwater. The average household throws away between 20 to 50 percent of items to landfills that are compostable.

Finally, businesses and landfills in many countries have experienced new regulations aimed to limit waste production. Some governments offer tax breaks to companies that utilize green behaviors and focus on waste reduction.

Recycling

Recycling is the act of repurposing trash materials that would have otherwise been discarded into a landfill. Discarded materials like paper, cardboard, metal, glass, wood, and plastic can often be used to make new items rather than extracting and utilizing raw materials to do so. This practice reduces waste and creates space in landfills, conserves materials like wood that are slow to renew, reduces methane production (therefore decreasing greenhouse gas production), and reduces energy production. Recyclable products can be sold domestically and globally, creating jobs and goods. Many residential and commercial buildings have municipal or county recycling services that will collect recycled items, similar to garbage collection. A number of chain grocery stores will take back plastic grocery bags for reuse. Cities, universities, airports, and other large domains are also making the practice of recycling more accessible by setting up single stream recycling containers in public locations, similar to garbage containers. Single stream recycling allows any recyclable material to be placed into the same container for collection. In previous years, consumers often had to separate recyclable goods themselves by material, which limited the number of people who chose to recycle. Products made from recycled materials are often noted as such. For example, cardboard food boxes, fast food napkins, paper towels, and soda cans often display information that they are made from previously recycled products, and from where the product was recycled (a program, a facility, or a consumer).

Environmentally Friendly Consumer Products

Environmentally friendly consumer products are those that are made from recycled components, or are biodegradable. *Biodegradable materials*, even in a landfill, will eventually completely organically decay over time. Environmentally friendly consumer products also refer to daily use household items that are made and utilized in a sustainable manner. For example, some toothpaste and soap manufacturers have removed certain chemicals and non-biodegradable plastics from their products, which consequently keeps plastics out of the soil system and the water supply. Some food companies produce only sustainable items, meaning that the production of the food is not depleting a natural ecosystem. Consumer demand for these types of products has increased greatly, and companies are trying to meet this demand. Eco-friendly companies not only produce environmentally friendly products, but also generally employ environmentally friendly manufacturing practices within their organizations.

Energy Production and the Management of Natural Resources

As the Earth's human population grows, more energy and natural resources are required to sustain communities. This need is increasing at a rate of approximately two-to-three percent annually. The growth in human population and related energy needs presents energy production and management issues that need to be addressed.

Renewable and Non-Renewable Energy Sources

Renewable energy sources are those that cannot be depleted; they are able to replenish themselves (or humans are able to replenish what they use) after consumption. These include sources such as solar energy, wind energy, hydro energy from the ocean, and geothermal heat. To be considered a viable resource, these energy sources should be able to translate into usable electricity, heat, cooling, or transportation fuel. Some biomass sources, such as waste, can also technically be considered "renewable" due to the amount of waste that humans produce. This would allow humans to recycle materials, and become less dependent on foreign fossil fuels. Scientists are also examining ways to make energy out of more plentiful biomass sources such as algae. Out of all human energy consumption in 2016, approximately one-fifth was from renewable resources. Out of all human energy production in 2016, approximately one-fourth was from renewable resources. Most large developed nations are investing heavily in renewable energy resources.

Traditionally, energy has come from *non-renewable energy sources* such as *fossil fuels* (common fossil fuels include carbon, coal, petroleum, oil, and natural gas) and other non-renewable biomass sources, such as wood. Fossil fuel consumption makes up almost three-fourths of all global energy consumption, with the United States responsible for almost twenty-five percent of that consumption. Fossil fuels take over millions of years to form, and supplies are quickly dwindling. Additionally, the methods of extracting fossil fuels are considered to be environmentally detrimental as is the exceedingly high production of greenhouse gases that results from their use. Fossil fuels are also concentrated in certain geographic locations around the globe, which has led to extensive geopolitical tension and conflict. These reasons have all led to the increased global interest in developing and utilizing renewable energy resources. However, barriers to developing renewable energy sources include those that are similar to any new start-up venture. Permitting, regulating, marketing to consumers, training employees, examining long-term implications, and costs are all barriers that are still being examined and managed.

Recycling and Conservation

Recycling and conservation are two important tools for protecting the Earth's resources, but as relatively newer practices, they are not without issues. In general, the practice of *recycling* allows for the *conservation* of Earth's resources by reusing manufactured products, which limits the production and use of raw materials. This reduces landfill use, minimizes waste elimination practices that release greenhouse gas emissions, and is often more cost-effective for manufacturers. However, introducing new recycling centers to an area is often costly in the beginning, as it requires constructing and developing the facility and hiring and training workers. Recycling facilities are often dirty, due to the nature of the items that are recycled, which may have once contained food items, human waste, and other organic materials. These materials quickly rot, may attract vermin, and/or create an overall biological hazard. If the waste from recycled materials is improperly handled, it can cause a pollution problem. Additionally, recycled materials used to create new goods may not be high quality, which can be problematic for the consumer. Finally, recycling is a newer trend that has not yet been adopted on a global scale. Some researchers worry that the amount of recycling that occurs is on a scale that is too small to have a lasting impact, and therefore may be a cost-prohibitive practice.

Pros and Cons of Power Generation

All presently available energy resources have pros and cons to their utilization. Fossil fuels are a non-renewable resource created from organic sources (such as coal) that developed over millions of years. Two pros for using fossil fuels include the existence of systems that are already in place to use this form of energy, and that a fairly large resource of fossil fuel material still exists. However, burning this resource for energy is a primary contributor to greenhouse gas production and disrupts many ecosystems. Sources are concentrated in certain areas around the globe, which has led to geopolitical conflict and tension. Additionally, the current rate of expenditure is faster than the rate of replenishment. This fact has led to research and development in the alternative energy industry.

Alternative energy sources include any source of energy that protects the environment and can be used as an alternative to fossil fuels. The term usually refers to solar, wind, water, and biomass power, but additional options also exist. In general, alternative energy sources are considered to be sustainable and conserving measures. However, a major con is that the industry is relatively new, and research is ongoing to utilize these sources in the most productive, efficient, and wide-reaching ways. Specific pros and cons of different types of alternative energy sources are listed below.

Nuclear fuel is a renewable resource created by the splitting of uranium atoms. This source greatly limits air pollution, as greenhouse gas emissions are low. Nuclear fuel also enjoys a relatively low production cost. However, upfront costs to build safe facilities are high. Nuclear accidents are also likely to be catastrophic to life, and adequate and safe storage of radioactive waste is another issue yet to resolve.

Hydropower refers to a renewable resource created from fast-flowing water sources that may be natural or man-made. This source is cheap, helps with global irrigation, and can provide drinking water. Disadvantages to hydropower include its inevitable disruption to many ecosystems; facilities are costly and may displace residents; and finally, while the risk of flooding is moderate, the risk of pollution is high.

Wind power refers to a renewable resource created by harnessing air flow. This source is abundant, cheap, clean, and does not require water or large facilities to use. However, wind has to be moving swiftly in order to be harnessed, and it cannot be stored. Commercializing a resource that easily crosses man-made borders can become complicated from legal and business standpoints.

Solar power is a renewable resource that uses the sun's rays for energy. This source is abundant, easily accessible, receives capital funding from both government and private sources, and requires minimal maintenance. However, even with subsidizing, initial production can be costly. It requires land or roof space for cell panels, and utilizes large-scale batteries. These can be a major contributor to waste and pollution.

Finally, *geothermal power* is a renewable resource that uses the Earth's core temperature to generate energy. This resource does not involve combustion (therefore no greenhouse gas emission), yet is three-to-five times more efficient than other sources. It can be used to heat or cool any residential or commercial space. However, utilizing this resource has a high upfront cost. It also requires a large amount of water, and can cause underground and well water damage. Additionally, emergency events, such as geyser eruptions and landslides, have a high risk of being catastrophic to life.

The Use and Extraction of Earth's Resources

Extracting resources from the Earth is inherently damaging in its process. *Mining* for minerals and fossil fuels has vast environmental impacts. Surface damage, unnatural erosion, increases in sinkholes, disruption to ecosystems, unnatural animal migration, and pollution are all side effects of mining. *Deforesting* lands to use the land for commercial or residential use or to use the trees for raw materials significantly disrupts ecosystems, contributes to global warming from reduced carbon dioxide consumption, affects water levels, reduces biodiversity, and endangers wildlife. Many rainforests, such as the Amazon rainforest, are believed to have "tipping points" of damage, where the land will be unable to replenish itself and the overall climate will have changed so drastically that it will set off other climate feedback responses. For example, cutting down trees leads to increased atmospheric carbon dioxide in the area, which leads to higher temperatures, which decreases plant water availability, resulting in less vegetation (and the loop continues). *Land reclamation* often focuses on correcting negative impacts to natural resources (i.e., restoring deforested lands by planting indigenous vegetation, replacing sands near beaches that have eroded, and so forth).

Applications of Science and Technology in Daily Life

Science and technology are a cornerstone of daily living, from influencing daily consumer products to the way people communicate with others. These fields aim to improve the daily standard and quality of living for the average person.

Chemical Properties of Household Products

Common household products such as cleaners, containers, and foods may be a source of toxic chemicals, especially to younger children. As a result, many companies have focused their efforts on developing clean, green household products that limit or eliminate the presence of common chemicals such as *phthalates, bisphenol A (BPA)*, and food preservatives that are increasingly becoming correlated to cancers, neurological dysfunction, hormone disruption, respiratory conditions, and endocrine issues. Additionally, many of these chemicals are also harmful to the environment when washed down drains; therefore, creating less toxic household products limits soil and water pollution as well.

Communication

The presence of the Internet, wireless networks, cell phones, online applications and social media, and global positioning systems (GPS) have paved the way for instantaneous, worldwide communication. These connections allow people to work and socialize remotely, navigate without maps, access hundreds of radio and television channels, and learn from and share vast pools of information. Additionally, large-scale two-way communication has become easier. An individual can connect with a large audience through the Internet alone, which has become a place to store and share documents, photos, videos, audio files, and more. All of these items were previously separate entities that could not be easily shared.

Science Principles Applied on Commonly Used Consumer Products

Most advances to average consumer products were first used by the scientific community for a much different purpose. For example, Teflon, the non-stick coating used in most pans that the average consumer uses to cook in the home, was originally created by a chemical engineer who was researching potential refrigerants. NASA has developed several mainstream products, such as infant formula, polarized sunglasses, and long-distance communication methods that initially were a part of space exploration research.

Water Purification

Water purification is an increasingly popular field as researchers hope to harness ocean water into potable water, purify available water in high pollution areas, and maintain increasingly stringent water purity standards. Previously, water had been primarily purified using filtration and chlorination. New water purification technologies include *membrane filtration* (which more finely filters water sources through pressurized, multiple, reverse osmosis processes), *ultraviolet radiation* (which works by sterilizing the water source), and more portable filtration systems that can be placed directly into a water source by the consumer.

Common Agricultural Practices

Agricultural practices have changed to keep up with population growth and land availability. *Genetically modified organisms (GMOs)* are those that have altered genetic coding to make them more resistant to harsh conditions and pests, or which can be grown in a lab under synthetic conditions. *Herbicides* and *insecticides* aim to eliminate common agricultural pests that destroy crops while leaving the crop intact. It is important to note that these are considered controversial practices by some consumers, who believe consumption of genetically modified food sources and the use of pesticides is linked to adverse health and environmental conditions.

DNA Evidence in Criminal Investigations

The last decade advanced the use of accurate *DNA profiling* and its ability to aid in forensic science and the judicial process. Current DNA profiling systems can match DNA samples taken from crime scenes to available DNA profiles in registered databases or from medical provisions. DNA profiling is considered to be more accurate than fingerprint testing or eyewitness testimony. It has been a fundamental tool in exonerating wrongly convicted criminals, and its present day use correlates with a reduction in overall crime rates. However, opponents argue that DNA profiling violates privacy rights and that human errors, false DNA samples, and synthetic DNA production can create inaccurate evidence.

Nanotechnology

Nanotechnology refers to new systems that result from manipulating material at the molecular level in order to create highly precise finished products. Scientists are able to use nanotechnology to change the composition of materials to make them stronger, lighter, more flexible, or able to withstand different chemical situations (such as rusting). Current nanotechnology initiatives include solar power cell manufacturing, developing medicines that can be administered at the cellular level, improving functionality of cell phones and other communication devices, removing contamination from water sources, and creating lighter yet larger memory storage (such as flash drives), space flight mechanisms, air quality improvement processes, and minute chemical detection.

Impact of Science on Public Health Issues

Science addresses many public health concerns, consequently leading to the eradication or sustainable management of diseases that were previously life-threatening. It has also made a notable impact on improving the overall quality of daily human life, such as helping infertile couples have children or providing means for disabled people to lead active lives.

Nutrition, Disease, and Medicine

Science has influenced a number of achievements in the fields of nutrition, disease, and medicine. Compounding synthetic vitamins, minerals, and other nutrients (such as collagen, amino acids, and fatty acids) provided a way for people with less access to nutrient-dense food sources or nutrition-related diseases to appropriately supplement their diets. Vaccine development has almost completely eradicated serious and crippling diseases like polio, diphtheria, tetanus, and pertussis; vaccines have also reduced the risk of contracting less fatal, but potentially critical, illnesses such as rotavirus and meningococcal viruses. As vaccines are administered in larger and larger groups, the risk of the bacterial or viral threat is greatly reduced. Even if a select few individuals are not vaccinated, the concept of herd immunity protects them and limits the spread of the threat. Other communicable diseases are now easily managed through the development and implementation of retroviral medications. *Retroviral drugs* can help people live full, normal lives with diseases like HIV, and such drugs have provided additional protection to pregnant mothers who can prevent passing a disease they have to their fetus. Overall, these advances have contributed to a reduction in child mortality rates and an increase in human life expectancy.

Here's an illustration of how vaccines decrease the spread of disease:

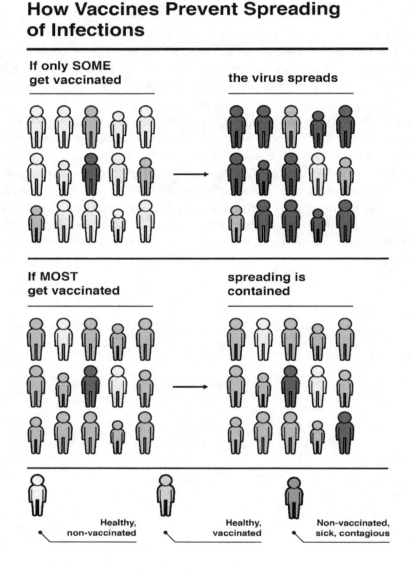

How Vaccines Prevent Spreading of Infections

If only SOME get vaccinated → **the virus spreads**

If MOST get vaccinated → **spreading is contained**

Healthy, non-vaccinated

Healthy, vaccinated

Non-vaccinated, sick, contagious

Biotechnology

The *biotechnology* field contributes to public health initiatives focused on genetic engineering, in vitro fertilization, infectious disease protection, and bioterrorist agent protection. Biotech companies contribute to the clinical development of vaccines and other pharmaceuticals and they create genetically modified crops that can withstand hazards that conventional crops may be unable to withstand. This is primarily accomplished through genome sequencing and mapping. Additionally, more biotech companies are being employed for national defense and security measures, as toxic bioterrorist agents, chemical warfare, and other risks to human biology can be used against the public. These defense measures include the development of enzymes that can neutralize threats, the development of internal barriers that protect an individual's cells from an approaching bacteria or virus, and refining DNA detection methods that show whether a population has been exposed to a biological threat.

Finally, biotech companies play a role in helping victims heal from various conditions. For example, some companies focus on creating realistic yet synthetic skin grafts to help burn victims return to normalcy.

Medical Technologies

Biomedical research and device manufacturing companies play a crucial role in advancing how medical professionals can detect, manage, and eliminate disease. The last century has delivered technological advances such as x-ray machines, electrocardiograms, medical imaging, and laparoscopic devices that allow medical professionals to visually and directly examine a patient's internal state, allowing for diagnoses with a high level of accuracy, and consequently, an effective treatment plan. Medical devices such as pacemakers, stents, dialysis machines, and catheters are able to carry on life-sustaining functions for an individual who has failing organs; sometimes these devices can be used for the rest of the patient's life. Artificial joints can be placed within a patient's skeletal system to replace failing or unusable joints, such as in the case of a hip or knee replacement. Current initiatives focus on virtual reality health delivery, augmented reality to deliver education for medical professionals, algorithm development and data analysis for data collected from popular individual fitness and wellness trackers, and the continued refinement of robotic assistance in medical centers and operating rooms. Finally, another type of technology to consider in medical contexts is the documentation process. The implementation of electronic medical records affects how healthcare is delivered, allowing for ease of communication between multiple providers and easier healthcare access for the patient. It is important to note, however, that the World Health Organization (WHO) reports that 70% of existing and emerging medical technologies cannot be used by developing nations due to reasons like lack of access, unskilled workers, and cultural fears.

Most medical technologies are developed in first-world, high income countries. Consequently, developing nations cannot access them, or do not have skilled workers to use the technologies appropriately. Additionally, some cultures do not accept foreign devices and reject them out of fear, misunderstanding, or disbelief. Consequently, many developing countries have poorer health outcomes, higher rates of disease, and lower life-expectancies because they are not benefiting from advancements in medical technology.

Practice Questions

1. Which period in history dramatically increased air, water, and soil pollution?
   a. The Paleolithic Era
   b. The Big Bang Era
   c. The Industrial Revolution
   d. The Medieval Ages

2. Which of the following is a man-made compound that is no longer approved for use due to its major detrimental effect on the ozone layer?
   a. Teflon
   b. Chlorofluorocarbons
   c. Carbon trioxide
   d. Fluorocarbon phosphates

3. Angie, a second-year college student, is visiting the Gulf Coast of Florida with an environmental conservation group for alternative spring break. The group's efforts focus on transporting truckloads of sand from various locations to a particular beach and creating dunes along some of the beach grasses. What conservation practice is this an example of?
   a. Deforestation
   b. Grassroots movement
   c. Reclamation
   d. Recycling

4. Which greenhouse gas is a common byproduct of landfills and concentrated animal feeding operations?
   a. Carbon
   b. Corn fumes
   c. Nitrogen
   d. Methane

5. The United States is responsible for what percentage of the total global fossil fuel consumption?
   a. 10%
   b. 15%
   c. 25%
   d. 30%

6. Which program is responsible for the research behind the development of a number of commonly used household items, such as infant formula?
   a. The Maternal, Child, and Infant Early Intervention Program
   b. The National Aeronautics and Space Administration Program
   c. The Department of Housing and Urban Development
   d. The Johnson Foundation Home Program

7. Which of the following resources are considered alternative energy sources?
   I. Wind power
   II. Hydroelectric power
   III. Wood
   IV. Algae power
   a. I and II
   b. I, II, III
   c. I, II, IV
   d. All of the above

8. Which of the following substances contributed to a lethal fog that spread over areas of England the United States in the mid-1900s, killing thousands and making many more critically ill?
   a. CFCs
   b. Smog
   c. Alkaline rain
   d. Cow manure

9. What percentage of medical technologies cannot be used by developing nations?
   a. 70%
   b. 80%
   c. 90%
   d. 100%

10. Which of the following is a condition that has been almost completely eradicated as a result of vaccination?
    a. Bubonic plague
    b. Polio
    c. HIV
    d. Chicken pox

11. A whooping cough outbreak occurs in a small town. The neighboring town's elementary school, which has 300 children enrolled, reviews their students' immunization records and notices all but four children have had the whooping cough vaccination. One year later, the outbreak in the area has been contained and no new cases have been reported in four months in the original town, as well as in its three neighboring towns. The elementary school notices it had no cases of whooping cough over the one-year period, including in the students who were not immunized against it. What is this likely an example of?
    a. Good sanitization practices
    b. Quarantine
    c. Herd immunity
    d. An argument against vaccinations

12. Which of these reasons may be a public benefit of producing genetically engineered crops?
    a. A monopoly on the production and distribution of the crops
    b. The crops can withstand harsh conditions, such as fluctuating temperatures and pesticides
    c. The concept promotes biodiversity
    d. The crops do not require any water

13. Geopolitical tension and conflict is associated with which of the following energy sources?
    a. Fossil fuels
    b. Nuclear power
    c. Wind power
    d. Natural gas

14. Which types of geological material can serve as natural filters for water?
    a. Clay and coal particles
    b. Leaf and limb particles
    c. Granite and quartz particles
    d. Shale and calcite particles

15. What percentage of the average household's trash could actually be composted, therefore reducing landfill usage?
    a. 10% to 20%
    b. 50% to 100%
    c. 5% to 25%
    d. 20% to 50%

Answer Explanations

1. C: The Industrial Revolution switched the economical focus for most of the world from agriculture to manufacturing. This period produced factories and many machines, which required the combustion of coal and other fuel sources. As a new industry, the lack of regulation did not combat the air pollution from these factories, nor were there rules on where to dump waste. While some pollution likely did occur in the other periods listed, the period of the Industrial Revolution, from approximately the mid-1760s to the early 1800s, caused a dramatic spike.

2. B: Chlorofluorocarbons (CFCs) were man-made compounds of chlorine, fluorine, and carbon used mainly in aerosol cans and refrigerants. Their use single-handedly caused significant depletion to the ozone layer, at a rate of about 20% globally and 70% over Antarctica. CFCs have mostly been banned from production, but it is unclear whether the ozone layer will ever reach pre-CFC usage levels. Teflon does not directly contribute to ozone layer depletion, and the other options listed are not real compounds.

3. C: Reclamation refers to making an area of defiled land usable by returning it to its natural state. In this instance, the spring break group is helping the shoreline by preventing further erosion from destroying the beach and its vegetation. Deforestation refers to removing vegetation. Grassroots movements typically refer to local, organized political movements. Recycling typically refers to repurposing a material that has already been consumed and making into another usable item.

4. D: Landfills and animal waste are large contributors to methane. They do not cause significant amounts of the other greenhouse gasses listed. Corn fumes are not a greenhouse gas.

5. C: The United States is the leading consumer of fossil fuels at 25% consumption, even though there are many other countries with higher populations.

6. B: The National Aeronautics and Space Administration Program (NASA) has conducted research for space exploration that has led to the development of commonly used household items. The Maternal, Child, and Infant Early Intervention program is a federal program focused on home visiting interventions. The Department of Housing and Urban Development focuses on providing housing to those who need assistance. The Johnson Foundation Home program is not a real program.

7. C: Alternative energy sources are those that can replace traditional energy sources such as fossil fuels. The term usually refers to solar, wind, water, and biomass power, but additional options, such as harnessing power from algae, also exist. Traditional energy sources are diminishing in quantity and are leading causes of pollution. Burning wood is not environmentally sustainable because it takes too long to replace.

8. B: Smog produced from organic, toxic compounds from factories so heavily blanketed areas in England and the United States that many suffocated or became violently ill. This eventually lead to air pollution initiatives. The other items listed did not play a role.

9. A: Most medical technologies are developed in first-world, high-income countries. Consequently, developing nations cannot access them, or do not have skilled workers to use the technologies appropriately. Additionally, some cultures do not accept foreign devices and reject them out of fear, misunderstanding, or disbelief. This is an issue as developing countries have poorer health statuses and health outcomes and could benefit from medical technology.

10. B: The polio vaccine has been the major contributor to polio eradication in the United States and in most countries worldwide. Only three countries continue to have polio epidemics. The bubonic plague does not have a vaccine and is not eradicated. HIV is managed with long-term retroviral drugs and has not been eradicated. Chicken pox can be prevented through vaccination but has not been eradicated.

11. C: The immunization of the majority of the community within the elementary school likely protected the four non-immunized students from contracting the disease, because the vaccinated students did not contract it and therefore could not spread it. The other options are highly unlikely or not mentioned in the case.

12. B: Genetically engineering crops can change their genetic sequencing to withstand harsh conditions and the pesticides used to treat pests that damage the crops. Choices A and C are reasons provided against the genetic engineering of crops by the practice's critics. Both genetically engineered and traditional crops require water.

13. A: Fossil fuels, like oil, are often concentrated in certain parts of the world. Some countries have access to them within their borders and import them at cost to other countries that are unable to access them. This is known to cause tension between countries and communities, as fossil fuels are a high-demand resource. This situation does not apply to the other energy sources listed.

14. A: Clay and coal particles are known for their filtration properties in aquifers, as they are porous enough to let water molecules through but keep debris from passing. The other items listed typically are not porous enough for adequate filtration; rather, they just block all water.

15. D: A large percentage of organic household items could be composted rather than be placed in landfills. Residential composting bins are becoming more popular in modern society, but could be advocated further as an easy way to reduce household waste.

Dear Praxis II General Science Test Taker,

We would like to start by thanking you for purchasing this study guide for your Praxis II General Science exam. We hope that we exceeded your expectations.

Our goal in creating this study guide was to cover all of the topics that you will see on the test. We also strove to make our practice questions as similar as possible to what you will encounter on test day. With that being said, if you found something that you feel was not up to your standards, please send us an email and let us know.

We would also like to let you know about other books in our catalog that may interest you.

Praxis II Elementary Education Test

This can be found on Amazon: amazon.com/dp/1628454326

Praxis II English Language Arts

amazon.com/dp/1628454105

Praxis II Social Studies

amazon.com/dp/1628454210

Praxis II Mathematics

amazon.com/dp/1628455624

Praxis Core Study Guide

amazon.com/dp/1628454946

We have study guides in a wide variety of fields. If the one you are looking for isn't listed above, then try searching for it on Amazon or send us an email.

Thanks Again and Happy Testing!
Product Development Team
info@studyguideteam.com

Interested in buying more than 10 copies of our product? Contact us about bulk discounts:

bulkorders@studyguideteam.com

FREE Test Taking Tips DVD Offer

To help us better serve you, we have developed a Test Taking Tips DVD that we would like to give you for FREE. **This DVD covers world-class test taking tips that you can use to be even more successful when you are taking your test.**

All that we ask is that you email us your feedback about your study guide. Please let us know what you thought about it – whether that is good, bad or indifferent.

To get your **FREE Test Taking Tips DVD**, email freedvd@studyguideteam.com with "FREE DVD" in the subject line and the following information in the body of the email:

     a. The title of your study guide.

     b. Your product rating on a scale of 1-5, with 5 being the highest rating.

     c. Your feedback about the study guide. What did you think of it?

     d. Your full name and shipping address to send your free DVD.

If you have any questions or concerns, please don't hesitate to contact us at freedvd@studyguideteam.com.

Thanks again!

CPSIA information can be obtained
at www.ICGtesting.com
Printed in the USA
LVHW06s1740280818
588398LV00025B/516/P

9 781628 455632